T0364639

DARK FEAR, EERIE CITIES

DARK FEAR, EERIE CITIES

New Hindi Cinema in Neoliberal India

ŠARŪNAS PAUNKSNIS

OXFORD
UNIVERSITY PRESS

OXFORD
UNIVERSITY PRESS

Oxford University Press is a department of the University of Oxford.
It furthers the University's objective of excellence in research, scholarship,
and education by publishing worldwide. Oxford is a registered trademark of
Oxford University Press in the UK and in certain other countries.

Published in India by
Oxford University Press
2/11 Ground Floor, Ansari Road, Daryaganj, New Delhi 110002, India

ISBN-13 (print edition): 978-0-19-949318-0
ISBN-10 (print edition): 0-19-949318-9

ISBN-13 (eBook): 978-0-19-909693-0
ISBN-10 (eBook): 0-19-909693-7

Typeset in Berling LT Std 9.5/14
by The Graphics Solution, New Delhi 110 092
Printed in India by Nutech Print Services India

To my family, for making this book possible

CONTENTS

ACKNOWLEDGMENTS

I must thank many people in different parts of the world for their help, support and advice through this journey. In Lithuania, I thank Ainius Lašas, Nerijus Čepulis, Eglė Butkevičienė, Saulius Keturakis and everyone at the Faculty of Social Sciences, Arts and Humanities, Kaunas University of Technology, Lithuania, for bearing with me while I was away in India for long months each year while writing this book. In India, I would like to thank Ira Bhaskar, Ranjani Mazumdar, Veena Hariharan, Kaushik Bhaumik, Rustom Bharucha, Shikha Jhingan, Yagati Chinna Rao, K.B. Usha, late Biswamoy Pati, Amrit Gangar and Ashish Avikunthak. Most of the writing of this book was done at Jawaharlal Nehru University (JNU), New Delhi, India. I thank Deepak Kumar and Raj Sekhar Basu for their friendship and for inviting me to JNU in 2013 and 2016 and G.J.V. Prasad for inviting me to Jawaharlal Nehru Institute of Advanced Study in 2017. My gratitude goes to my teachers Rachel Dwyer (SOAS University of London, UK) and Sudipta Kaviraj (Columbia University, New York, USA) and to my friend Hans Harder of Heidelberg University, Germany, who has been my constant support.

Last but not the least, I want to thank my family. My parents, without whose support and understanding this journey would not have been possible, and my companion, my wife Runa, with whom I started sharing this life while the book was being written and whose intellectual and emotional support, suggestions and love helped me complete this project.

INTRODUCTION

Madhur Bhandarkar's film *Page 3* (2005) starts with an illuminating scene. A non-resident Indian (NRI) businessman, who has just returned to India from the United States with an aim to invest, is hiring a public relations firm to help him in creating his image. The best strategy, according to the firm's representatives, is to organize lavish parties, invite celebrities and wealthy businessmen and hire the media to cover the event by printing photos of it in the gossip section of a newspaper known as "Page 3". The film contains several important elements: the figure of the NRI businessman as one who has returned to India ready to invest in a newly liberalized economy, the power of media and advertisement, but above all, the shifting cultural atmosphere of the 1990s and early 2000s—something that is crucial for this book as well.

This book is devoted to some of the key aspects of "new Hindi cinema"—a film form found in Hindi language films that are produced in Mumbai. New Hindi cinema began to emerge in the early 2000s, and marked a departure from the dominant cinematic esthetics in what is often called Bollywood. The aspects that are so prominent in Hindi cinema nowadays are what I call dark aspects: films focusing on the "dark side" of urban life, on crime, on the insecurity one is bound to feel while living in a metropolis—physical insecurity as well as a psychological insecurity of competition, a desire to succeed, to become successful and to belong to a newly emergent middle class.

On the one hand, we can see certain desires emerging, not necessarily new, but definitely strengthened and transformed by the new socio-political logic—a desire for a successful career, to belong to the middle class, to own certain goods signifying belonging to a certain category of society and to have a lifestyle that speaks of success. Such desires, as I argue throughout the chapters in this book, face different obstacles and I am mostly interested in how these obstacles are imagined in cinema. Cinema can perhaps be seen as mirroring the unconscious and as a means to channel out the conflict, perhaps in a similar way to psychoanalysis. Therefore, the film form I am discussing in this book maps the unconscious of India after the economic liberalization in the early 1990s, or what I call a neoliberal India.

I began this project trying to understand why the change has happened, why the new esthetics started to gradually gain ground, and by 2018, became dominant in mainstream cinema in Hindi. What happened in the early 2000s? In the book, I take the economic processes starting in the late 1980s as the watershed moment and explain the rise of new cultural sensibilities as the outcome of economic liberalization, which formally started in 1991. By taking the step to liberalize the economy, India opened itself up for global capitalism, which had a tremendous impact on almost all spheres of life and, most importantly, gave rise to new cultural sensibilities and shifting perceptions of self, of Other, of life and of the world. While, as I claim, the 1990s, looking at the cinematic representations, was a period of euphoric joy regarding becoming global, the rhetoric becomes far more pessimistic and, indeed, dark and eerie in the 2000s. The rise of new Hindi cinema's dark vision of urban India is similar to other cinematic forms that have emerged in different parts of the world after various crises, most notably, the rise of what is termed as "film noir" in mid-20th-century United States—a film form adopting a bleak and cynical position toward the urban space it is set in, narrated by a lonely man, who is often a private detective trying to solve a crime. As I explain in Chapter 4, film noir was influenced by a certain social context of post-War America and later became one of the most dominant film forms globally, various aspects of which are adopted by different film-makers in many cinemas worldwide. India is no exception, and the adoption of a bleak and cynical approach toward various aspects of urban life is at the core of new Hindi cinema. The logic, representational problems and philosophy of film noir is a thread that runs throughout the book.

The aim of this book is to look at new Hindi cinema from several angles—from the urban space and urban culture of emergent upper-middle classes and from the pessimism and alienation most films are infused with. Why is there so much pessimism? What impact does neoliberalism have on the city and cinematic representations? Why does the darkness—actual and metaphorical—proliferate? What haunts the city and why? Why is the city so dark and eerie? What happens to man in such a space? What many of the new Hindi cinema films share is the feeling of the uncanny, and this Freudian concept, which I explain in Chapter 3, is one of the central ones in this book. In trying to tackle these questions, in Chapter 1, I look at the methodological problems arising from understanding new Hindi cinema as a cinematic phenomenon. What is "new" in new Hindi cinema? How should we understand the emergence of this film form? Is it a mere extension of indie cinema or is it something else? Is it a part of Bollywood or is it outside of it? Chapter 2 looks at the problem of the urban center and the periphery as well as the production of the Other in neoliberal India and new Hindi cinema. The Other here means one that is outside of the new emergent middle class. It can be a rural otherness but often it is the urban, deprived lower orders of the society. Chapters 3 and 4 deal with the problem of the urban uncanny from the perspectives of horror cinema and film noir, respectively. One of the key features of new Hindi cinema is the transforming approach to gender and the representation of a crisis-stricken, anxious man trying to survive in a changing world. Chapter 5 looks at the representation of men in new Hindi cinema and the rise of masculine anxiety and its critique on screen.[1] Indeed, one thread that runs through the chapters of this book is the performativity of masculinity in

---

[1] Some of the material used in this book has been published earlier. Please refer to Paunksnis (2014, 2015, 2015/2016, 2016a, 2016b, 2017).

neoliberal age. While the object of this forms the core of the last chapter, dark undertones in cinematic imagination of neoliberal India generally relate to embodiments of maleness and various trajectories and meanings of being a man. As I shall demonstrate, film noir has always worked through masculine anxiety or protest masculinity—an important element that new Hindi cinema inherits from the classical film noir as an expression of unconscious struggles. The book looks at various aspects of masculine anxiety. But space is another important keyword in the book—amorphous, transforming urban spaces, conflictual relationships with (neo)liberal ethics, visualizations and embodiments of "man in his space" and man in "alienated space". Film noir as a form, essentially, is about pain, wounds and scarring. A scarred male is a male wounded by a woman, by economic impotence or financial pressures to succeed, to be one's inventor and entrepreneur. Such psychological and sociological problems are central to neoliberal ontology. They inform new imagination in Hindi cinema, the visualization and imagining the individual in the 21st century Indian city and the desires of the middle class to become global. As I shall demonstrate in the last part of the book, following Alfred Adler (1956), protest masculinity can be either male or female; it is not gender-bound—a woman can rebel against patriarchy and, in the anti-feminist nightmare, transform into a castrating female, a vengeful woman who is, ambiguously, admired and detested. In order to unpack and to deconstruct the cultural shifts, I work through cinema not as a film scholar but as a cultural critic, which gives me a much wider perspective. This book should not be understood as a "film studies" book but as a much broader investigation in the philosophy and sociology of transforming neoliberal India.

According to Arvind Rajagopal (2008: 1), "Hindu Nationalism represented an attempt to fashion Hindu public within the nexus of market reforms and the expansion of communications." What nationalism and neoliberalism have in common are the desires to refashion society, to produce a new individual, indeed, a new human being, new sensibilities and new points of reference in understanding the world. As Comaroff and Comaroff (2001: 13) put it, neoliberal culture "is a culture that … re-visions persons not as producers from a particular community, but as consumers in a planetary marketplace: persons as ensembles of identity that owe less to history or society than to organically conceived human qualities". Both nationalism and neoliberalism in India "drew on market forces energized in the process of neoliberalization, on the support of middle classes asserting their newly legitimated right to consume and of business groups seeking a successor to a developmentalist regime in eclipse" (Rajagopal 2008: 1).

The initial phase of liberalization was marked by the importance of NRI Indians, their support for the shifting policies as well as their support for the political power strongly advocating the transformations—the Bharatiya Janata Party (BJP), which rose to prominence precisely during the 1980s. The coming of neoliberalism, therefore, was marked by a liberalizing market allowing foreign investments, including ones by the NRIs and, simultaneously, by the increasing importance of Hindu nationalism, propagated by the BJP and the right-wing nationalist network of Sangh Parivar that the BJP belongs to. Projecting itself as a flag-bearer of progress—progress here meaning a pro-business, pro-free market one—and banking on the support from wealthy NRIs in the United States, United Kingdom and elsewhere, the BJP not only managed to implement the neoliberal agenda but also a nationalist one. The story of neoliberalism as a kind of "market fundamentalism" in India is inseparable from the story of Hindu fundamentalist revival. This should not be surprising. On a global scale, neoliberal reforms in the 1980s were being promoted by some of the most conservative politicians, like US President Ronald Reagan and UK Prime Minister Margaret Thatcher. So, neoliberalism as a kind of "market fundamentalism" was conveniently going hand in hand with different other types of political fundamentalisms—be it conservative forces in the United States or the United Kingdom or Hindu fundamentalism in India. Neoliberalism, an economic doctrine, has had a significant, if not decisive, effect on social, political, cultural and economic developments globally since the 1970s. Neoliberalism has never been purely about the economy—it always had a far more ambitious project of remaking the humanity and giving birth to a new human being: *homo oeconomicus*. Culture, therefore, is of massive significance to neoliberalism. It is not only important what

individuals *do* in the market or what market *does* to an individual but
also the remaking of the value system. Neoliberalism may be "the
pursuit of disenchantment of politics by economics," but at the same
time, it is also a re-enchantment (Davies 2014). Neoliberalism strives
to forge a new subject and a new experience of phenomena, as many
scholars have demonstrated (Brown 2003, 2015; Harvey 2007). Dardot
and Laval (2014: 288) call this new/neoliberal subject a "neo-subject",
and claim that "we are no longer dealing with old disciplines intended
to train bodies and shape minds through compulsion to render them
more submissive". What has changed, according to them, is the forging
of "desire to realize oneself" in the production of the neoliberal subject,
which is shaped as an entrepreneurial subject. What is manufactured
is the desiring subject—desiring to succeed, to be efficient, to be a self-
contained enterprise. Neoliberalism in this sense becomes the Other
and, therefore, as Dardot and Laval (2014: 289) claim, "the desire of
the subject is the desire of the Other". However, such desires that the
neo-subject nurtures have dark sides and, as I shall demonstrate later,
can be the sources of neurosis, of fears and anxieties that manifest
themselves in various ways.

Neoliberalism in India underwent a "second coming" in 2014 with
the overwhelming rise to power of the BJP, under the leadership of
Narendra Modi, both on the national and local political levels. Once
again, we are able to see the increasing promotion of neoliberal policies
and maxims (for example, "India Shining" becomes "Make in India").
Current political and economic changes undoubtedly are having effects
on culture in India but it is not the aim of this book to discuss them.
Transformations of fears and anxieties that are channeled out of the
social unconscious by cinema will take time to manifest themselves,
although some effects on film production are visible today, mostly
relating to increasing censorship and negative effects on film-makers'
freedom of speech. However, this would be a theme for another and a
very different book. It is not the aim of this book to investigate what
kind of neoliberal subjects are produced in India or to try to answer
questions related to who is a neoliberal subject or what sort of subject
that is. I am not aiming at explaining the cultural logic of neoliberalism

in India. Other authors, whom I mention throughout this book, have been preoccupied with such questions for a long time. Neoliberal rationality, the rise of the new middle class, new form of cultural distinction and subject formation are considered as a background against which the new imagination is taking shape. My focus is on certain themes in cinema that I hold to be central and crucial in understanding the emergence of the neoliberal self.

Economic liberalization caused massive commodification in the cultural field as well as the emergence of new cultural formations, new dreams and new aspirations. Liberalization caused the emergence of Bollywood itself—an industry *selling dreams* and comprised of films, star culture, shifts in film production, financing, distribution and advertising. This period also saw the emergence of cable and satellite television, which, in tandem with Bollywood, has contributed to the emergence of new subjectivities. The transformations resulted in varied manifestations of the "global", but more precisely hybrid cultural formations. Middle classness is one particular sensibility that has emerged. It is a subject of neoliberalism in India, and in the case of this book—crucial in terms of consumption of new Hindi cinema and in terms of being represented in most of the films discussed.

Middle Classness in Neoliberal India

Instead of a more specific term "middle class", which points toward specific groups and is commonly used in this case, I am inclined to use the term "middle classness", following Leela Fernandes (2006). As she puts it, "the image of the new middle class represents an idealized national standard of living that other social groups can aspire to and potentially achieve through the practices of consumption" (Fernandes 2006: 32).

Fernandes (2006: 30), in defining the new Indian middle class, states that it "represents a hegemonic sociocultural embodiment of India's transition to a committed liberalizing nation". She also draws upon the spatial reorganization practices developing "new suburban identities that seek to displace visual signs of poverty from public spaces"

(Fernandes 2006: xxii). Brosius (2013, 2014) makes similar arguments on the new middle class, as do Athique and Hill (2010) in their study on the rise of the multiplex in India. Neoliberalism in India has created spaces not belonging to "shining" neoliberal India: spaces that reflect the myth of everything the "new" self is not; spaces of radical alterity; spaces that are beyond psychic interaction despite the fact of physical proximity. New cinema, a peculiar film form as part of new India's visual culture, is instrumental both in constructing and representing the new spatial dichotomies as well as the dichotomies of self and Other. In new spatial imagination, more often than not, otherness manifests itself as a formless outside space infused with fear, violence and barbarity—a heterotopian space of a North Indian village. This village has acquired a very different symbolic status in India of the new middle class. No longer is it a nostalgic space of origin—an imagination that dominated in the postcolonial period in India. No longer can it be associated with safe and serene space; it is a space of its opposite, of the uncanny. The North Indian village as a heterotopian space with a clear function in modern imaginary has transformed from an idyllic space of Indianness to an uncanny space of the Other. The foreignness of the Nehruvian and early post-Nehruvian period became reterritorialized as a homelier ontological space than the villages of a distant and semi-mythic past. New sexualities and individualism, consumerism and McDonaldization, shopping malls as spatial markers of new identity, democracy and capitalism became the new mental spaces and new imaginary territories of neoliberal India, a spectatorial milieu casting its "enclaved gaze" toward the *mofussil* and rural India, in the words of Brosius (2013), and trying to negotiate its newness vis-à-vis the past, which still haunts, as a repressed trauma one cannot negate. Some of the new Hindi cinema films reflect what I would later call neurotic realist imagination, like *NH10* (Navdeep Singh, 2015) and *Highway* (Imtiaz Ali, 2014)—films that are a good evocation of mental and actual spaces of the self, positioned vis-à-vis uncanny heterotopian emplacements of the Other. Middle classness, as any sensibility and world view, is also a spatial practice and is determined by materiality of space and the conditions of existence. Space mediates the construction of perceptions and attitudes inasmuch as it is produced by them. It is useful to understand the sum of society and space as *habitus* (Bourdieu 1977). Habitus, a necessarily social space, cultivates what Shields (1991: 52–3) terms as "spatial competence". It produces habits, manners and rituals related to space (for example, performance in a shopping mall). Space is produced in using it, in interacting with it as well as in relation to other spaces. Transforming film esthetics must be understood as a part of the habitus of new urban middle classes, as a reflection of new, emergent spatial competence.

Christiane Brosius (2014: 1), commenting on the "Shining India" election campaign launched by the BJP in 2004 and the enthusiasm that the slogan was met with, states that "to many of them, 'India Shining' is another term associated with the desire and ability to enjoy and move forward into a new world, a world full of light, comfort and prosperity". Enthusiasm in mainstream Hindi cinema was felt even before that. Cinematic India was already "shining" in mid- to late-1990s, especially in Aditya Chopra's and Karan Johar's films. They were imagining a rich, upper class "global" India and, at the same time, a highly patriarchal and hierarchic one. Mainstream Bollywood, however, transformed in the post-"India Shining" years.[2] Despite the imagination of good life, comfort and "world classness" as aspirational goals, which necessarily are globalized dreams (for example, highly popular films like Zoya Akhtar's *Zindagi Na Milegi Dobara* [2011] and *Dil Dhadakne Do* [2015]), the imaginary world of cinema has become less full of visions of "light, comfort and prosperity" than ever before (Brosius 2014: 1). It is haunted by anxiety stemming from what Srivastava (2014: 143) in his analysis of transforming urban space in Delhi called "the nightmare of Indian realities". Such anxiety, as I shall demonstrate in this book, is one of the central features of the cinema in question. Some films, like *NH10* or *Highway*, directly engage with this; some are the products of haunting, like Anurag Kashyap's films. The story of

---

[2] A good example can be Karan Johar's changed tone starting with *Kabhi Alvida Naa Kehna* (2006) through *My Name Is Khan* (2010) to *Student of the Year* (2012).

urban transformations informs the story of so-called urban cinema—it is impossible to understand the new Hindi cinema without understanding the transforming urban space, the question of dwelling in this space and the neoliberal logic driving the transformation. The cinema discussed in this book can be seen as urban cinema—art, commodity and a site of cultural negotiation, complacency and critique deeply related to neoliberal logic.

This book is about the emergence of new sensibilities but, more than that, it is about the critique of such sensibilities, the dark side of neoliberal sensibilities and the manifestations of the darkness as an after-effect of neoliberal politics and culture.

I

UNDERSTANDING CINEMATIC TRANSFORMATIONS AND NEOLIBERAL CULTURE IN INDIA

Saajan Fernandes, the protagonist of Ritesh Batra's *The Lunchbox* (2013), rides in an auto-rickshaw at night through the streets of Mumbai, looking at the brightly lit windows of shops selling branded goods. In an off-screen monologue, in the form of a letter he is composing to Ila, a woman he has never met, he ponders on the transforming space of his city and the disappearance of certain key spaces of his past. With melancholy in his voice, he says:

> The old houses of boys I used to play with when I was a child are gone now. My old school too. Some things are still the same. The old post office—still there. And the hospital where I was born and where my parents died, and my wife. I think we forget things if we have no one to tell them to.

Paul Virilio (2005: 105) in *Negative Horizon* writes:

> The ground [fond] of the landscape rises up to the surface, inanimate objects are exhumed from the horizon and come each in turn to permeate the glaze of the windscreen, perspective becomes animated, the vanishing point becomes a point of attack sending forth its lines of projection on to the voyeur–voyageur, the objective of the continuum

becomes a focal point that casts its rays on the dazzled observer, fascinated by the progression of landscapes. The generative axis of an apparent movement materializes suddenly through the speed of the machine, but this concretization is totally relative to the moment, for the object that hurls itself upon the layer of the windscreen will also be as quickly forgotten as perceived, stored away in the prop room, it will soon disappear in the rear window.

Virilio developed the concept of dromology, "a science of speed", and throughout his body of work, is concerned about our transforming relationship with phenomena in an age variously referred to as postmodern or late capitalist, hyper-industrial or liquid modern. In *The Lunchbox*, Saajan, similarly to Virilio, observes the transforming city and the disappearances that keep on occurring—disappearing spaces, disappearing people, disintegration of intimacy and the semi-real, semi-imaginary relationships one forges with people who, otherwise, are ungraspable, inapproachable and transient. The city in this film, as in many others that shall be discussed in this book, is the main source of imagination, of imagining the global, of sophistication and squalor. It is an object of inquiry as much as it always is a leading protagonist. Virilio, who, besides being a philosopher is also an urban planner and architect, writes of an increasing speed of life, technological and televisual, and its impact on our perceptions of phenomena. He is interested in the loss of capability to perceive when we are deprived of the usual tools for perception and experience; when the tools are transformed, deformed and unrecognizable, making our spatial experience alienating. He is concerned with the rapidly shifting relationship of individuals to a place, and emphasizes the emergence of a so-called world-city, or global city, and the transforming effect on relationships it imposes on those who dwell there (Virilio 2008: 71). The movement produced by speed—the speed of urban transformation, of life in a metropolis—is so fast that the environment around us loses its contours and its colors: the world surrounding us becomes gray, blurred and imposes an impossibility to distinguish features or distinct objects. As an antidote to this, Virilio advocates a gray ecology, which is a concern with pollution of a different kind, "a dromospheric pollution … that attacks liveliness of the subject and the mobility of the object by atrophying the journey to the point where it becomes needless" (Virilio 2008: 33–4). A journey on a high-speed train and an ability to see only the blurred objects outside the window is an example that he gives. For him, the televisual speed—the speed introduced by cinema—forms one of the key issues alienating individuals from direct experience of phenomena. The speed of images flashing before our eyes and the bodily speed we experience are closely related and inform one another. Experience of the phenomena in such a case is transforming too. The experience itself signifies difference—difference of perception, difference of relating to things and people. Saajan observes the transforming Mumbai as if from a distance—from an auto-rickshaw, from a train, from his terrace, from the emotional and physical detachment of a lonely middle-aged man. The intimacy he manages to forge is with a woman who, for him, exists only in brief letters and in food delivered to him daily; intimacy for him is squarely a media experience of an early 21st-century Indian city. Saajan's transformed city is a memory map, a city trying to forget its past in order to emerge as a "world city", as a post-urban space (Vidler 1994: 185–6). Saajan longs for the past, attempts to remember the intimate spaces and experiences—spaces of his childhood as well as the intimacy of home, when his wife was still alive. *The Lunchbox*, among other films, ponders on the homesickness in a post-urban space, in a city that has moved on, erasing the markers of history and selfhood—such breaks with the past and history are part of the neoliberal urban transformations, where non-places and other ghostly spaces come to dominate the map (Bauman 2000; Augé 2008; Cheung 2009). *The Lunchbox* is a melancholic film interrogating loneliness in big city. It also shows loneliness at home, in an intimate space one can no longer relate to, hence, dreaming of semi-real, heterotopian emplacements—to use Michel Foucault's (2000) notion—like Bhutan, where, as Ila and Saajan imagine, life may be happier. The film also represents material spaces so central to contemporary urban India—offices, commuter trains, houses where one only comes to sleep. Houses, not homes. Gaston Bachelard (1994: 8), emphasizing the importance of intimate space of a house that is a home, coined the term of topoanalysis, a "systematic psychological study of the sites of our intimate lives". He explores the houses of our past, of our childhood, containing memories and intimacy—spaces that constitute a significant part of our selves and produce what he terms as "topophilia"—sentiments related to a place. The transformation or disappearance of such homely, serene and safe spaces results in the fundamental shifts in perception of phenomena, new emergent sensibilities, new pathways in identity formation or singularization (Guattari 2000; Stiegler 2014). Or, paraphrasing Martin Heidegger (1968), spatial transformations produce spaces in which *dwelling* does not occur. However, dwelling is attempted to construct "within an environment of 'placelessness' and alienation", as Shields (1991: 15) argues, but this has further implications in terms of *spatial perceptions*, as I shall demonstrate.

What's in a Name?

The deterioration of our ability to grasp phenomena, to relate intimately to things and spaces and the urgency to produce space out of non-places, in the words of Marc Augé (2008), are among the developments demarcating the times of rapid social and spatial transformations, and in our case, the transformations in post-liberalization India of the late 20th to early 21st century. Such deterioration of perception abilities, or perhaps speedy transformation of such abilities, leaving them beyond conventional tools of perception, mark transformations of cinema as well. In my opinion, the discussions on current cinematic transformations in Hindi cinema and different ways to approach, compartmentalize and understand the cinematic phenomena are indicators of the transient nature of our perception. Research on current transformations of Hindi cinema is emerging, and different scholars provide different explanations of transforming Hindi cinema and different terminologies facilitating or, perhaps, taming the unruly artistic form (Gopal 2011; Dwyer 2013, 2016; Gehlawat 2015; Devasundaram 2016). In my view, current debates may be counter-productive, as they attempt to use conventional tools, that is, use of concepts like "Bollywood" and "indie", "mainstream" and "art house" and so on. It is convenient to place the emergent cinematic forms into binary categories erected before these transformations even began, but this may lead to serious problems and simplify their understanding. On the one hand, I see the current transformations as spontaneous rhizomatic formations defying strict and binary categorization. At the same time, even working within the conventional understanding of cultural change, we may problematize the "newness" in a more cautious and perhaps more pessimistic manner. The most important question I would like to address in this chapter relates precisely to conceptualization and theoretical location of cinematic transformations.

New cinematic esthetics, a highly diverse rhizomatic film form, began to emerge in the early 2000s. Some of the films marking the start of the flow (although, as always, it is hard to pinpoint the first film or films) may be *Chandni Bar* (Madhur Bhandarkar, 2001), *Being Cyrus* (Homi Adajania, 2005), *Manorama Six Feet Under* (Navdeep Singh, 2007) and *Rang De Basanti* (Rakeysh Omprakash Mehra, 2006), among many others. These shifts were influenced by the "alternative" within Bollywood that existed in the 1990s, best exemplified by the Mumbai underworld films of Ram Gopal Varma, like *Satya* (1998). On the other hand, the new forms were influenced by the existing indie cinema, like *Hyderabad Blues* (Nagesh Kukunoor, 1998) or *Bombay Boys* (Kaizad Gustad, 1998). This form can incorporate films and filmmakers as diverse as Vishal Bhardwaj, Anurag Kashyap, Anand Gandhi and Prakash Jha, among others. Rachel Dwyer (2013) aptly proposes to locate this diversity in a spectrum, where at one end, one could place a more commercial cinema (for example, Vishal Bhardwaj, Prakash Jha and Rakeysh Omprakash Mehra), and on the other, more offbeat cinema that is oriented toward a smaller niche audience, for example, earlier works of Dibakar Banerjee, like *Khosla ka Ghosla* (2006), *Oye Lucky, Lucky Oye!* (2008) and *Love, Sex aur Dhokha* (2010), or some relatively recent works like *Ship of Theseus* (Anand Gandhi, 2013), *The Lunchbox* (Ritesh Batra, 2013), *Titli* (Kanu Behl, 2014) or *Masaan* (Neeraj Ghaywan, 2015).

Dwyer proposes several terms as ways of understanding the new cinematic phenomenon—*hatke* [different] (Dwyer 2013) and "middlebrow" (Dwyer 2016). She sees the middlebrow as a wide spectrum that can accommodate the multiplicity of forms and cinematic expressions without clear categorization of cinema into mainstream and art. For her, Aamir Khan's films like *PK* (Rajkumar Hirani, 2014), *3 Idiots* (Rajkumar Hirani, 2009) or *Taare Zameen Par* (Aamir Khan, 2007) can function as a kind of "upper middlebrow", a more commercial variant of middlebrow cinema, while the vast category she is using can accommodate far less mainstream films like Anurag Kashyap's films, including his early, far less commercially oriented work like *Paanch* (2003, unreleased) and *Black Friday* (2004) (Dwyer 2016). In a similar vein, Sangeeta Gopal (2011: 14) uses a term "New Bollywood", and claims, that "New Bollywood ... refers to the entire world of cinema—industrial practices, financing, exhibition, audience, tie-ins, and of course the films themselves—of the post-liberalization period" (1991–present)". Her definition contradicts Vasudevan's, who states that Bollywood is precisely the product of post-liberalization, global age, and therefore Bollywood is inherently new (Vasudevan 2010: 339–46). My understanding on the new lies in further and deeper transformation in the 2000s, particularly in the emergence of new sensibility strongly influenced by noir esthetics and dirty realist imagination, as I shall discuss later. Newness in this case is signified by emergent pessimism, bleakness and in some cases, irony, all focused on the problems of urban dwelling, relationship with India outside the globalized dream worlds, and how the outside informs and shapes the shifting understanding of the neoliberal self.

What all these films and filmmakers have in common is an esthetic departure from cinematic forms that dominated Hindi cinema for decades—what Vasudevan (2010) calls a melodramatic form, or what M. Madhava Prasad (2000) identifies as "feudal family romance". The new form often tends to focus on the "other side" of India, of neoliberal progress and affirmative globalization—dehumanizing urbanism; rural slums, small towns and villages no longer perceived as a space of origin, no longer filled with nostalgia; and brutality and drama of life more generally. Often these films portray the middle class in crisis or focus on life other than the urban middle class, in short, on the new middle class's Other—the Other not (yet) admitted to enjoy the pleasures and pains of neoliberal living.

The new cinematic esthetics cater to urban, multiplex-going middle classes, Indian diasporas abroad as well as non-Indian "world" cinema aficionados. Emergent esthetic difference, whether we call it middlebrow cinema, New Bollywood or indie, has its epistemological problems that can be excavated by employing a complex theoretical framework. One issue most scholars writing on Hindi cinema agree on is the overlapping of mainstream and art. On the one hand, seeing newness as a rhizomatic formation can be enlightening, but at the same time, the collapse of neat categorization can signify far more grim cultural processes.

Studying Cinema, Cultural Transformations and Neoliberalism

Steven Shaviro (2010: 36), writing on French filmmaker Olivier Assayas' "post-cinema" states the following:

> The space of transnational capital is at the same time extremely abstract, and yet suffocatingly close and intimate. On the one hand, it is so abstract as to be entirely invisible, inaudible, and intangible.... For this space is a relational one, largely composed of, and largely shaped by, the arcane financial instruments, and other transfers of "information," that circulate through it. These instruments and flows, and the trans-actions in the course of which they are exchanged, cannot be "repre-sented" in any form accessible to the human senses; they can only be defined computationally, as the terms of utility functions and partial differential equations.

Hindi cinema of the 21st century is preoccupied with representation of the spaces affected and transformed by transnational capital. Following Fredric Jameson's (1991) claim that the transnational capitalism is unrepresentable, Shaviro (2010) analyzes the problem of represent-ing what cannot be represented, or making visible what is invisible. Such representation is very problematic if the problem of neoliberal-ism, globalization or transnational capitalism is approached directly. Neoliberalism is composed of financial flows, transactions, invest-ments—abstractions impossible to be represented as such. In order to be representable, the abstraction and virtuality of neoliberalism has to be embodied, allegorically and materially, as an effect of neoliberalism. In cinema, neoliberalism is most effectively embodied spatially, using space both as a metaphor and as material space. Space, which is transient, affected by neoliberalism and undergoes transformation, can be seen as a dominant chronotope in Hindi cinema since the 1990s, to use Mikhail Bakhtin's (1981) concept of a time-space that links the world represented in the work of art and the real world. Chronotope can be understood as a pattern in terms of what material conditions in a certain historical period are represented and in what way. In Bakhtin's case—also in a particular genre. Such material spaces in Hindi cinema, certain locations, certain spaces that proliferate, where the individuals act and dwell, spaces where they interact with each other as well as with spaces are the emergent non-places of transnational capitalism, such as shopping malls, multiplexes, luxury apartment buildings and gated communities. Also, streets, marginal and liminal spaces of pavements, narrow lanes and slums and dingy apartments where individuals negotiate their identities and interact with the abstract flows of capital and the flows of newness.

Vivian Sobchack (1998) in her influential essay on film noir juxtaposes the spatial or architectural anxiety of noir with Bachelard's intimate space of a home. She rightly asserts the nostalgia for intimacy as nostalgia for the past that Bachelard's text evokes—intimacy that is yet hard to recognize and *produce* in a transformed social as well as urban space. In understanding cinema's interaction with real, material space, she uses the concept of chronotope. Her "adaptation" of the Bakhtinian concept for film analysis is useful in looking at spatial representations and the interaction of real world, real space and the space represented in films. A city generally can be seen as a chronotope having a certain pattern of representation since the 1990s in Hindi cinema. But it is smaller chronotopes that are more relevant—in urban India's case—a street, a shopping mall, a luxury apartment and the relationship individuals have with these spaces, and with each other in these spaces.

The political alliance between Hindu nationalism and neoliberal forces reshaped the perceptions of social life, and this shift in points of reference and transformations of sensibilities is visible in the popular

Hindi cinema of the 1990s, especially in films starring Shah Rukh Khan, evoking a "global", upper-middle-class male, a citizen of the world, as it were, but at the same time—with a very clear-cut understanding of "Indianness", which more often than not manifested itself as subservience and indeed a reaffirmation of the Hindu patriarchic order. Many examples illuminating this can be found in Bollywood films of the 1990s—a cinematic period that essentially tried to articulate transforming cultural, social and political plateaus. Some examples may be *Dilwale Dulhania Le Jayenge* (Aditya Chopra, 1995), a film that inaugurated the new upper-middle-class "global" Indianness, *Kuch Kuch Hota Hai* (Karan Johar, 1998) and very importantly *Kabhi Khushi Kabhie Gham* (Karan Johar, 2001). *Kabhi Khushi Kabhi Gham*, boasting of a cast of *who's who of Bollywood*, affirms the submission to patriarchic Hindu authority, to global capital and to the nation simultaneously, as well as a woman's submission to a man.

Post-1990s can be seen as a more confident neoliberal period, a period when the sensibilities of what Fernandes calls "middle classness" became more entrenched, less amorphous. It was also a period when the spatial reconfigurations became more prominent. Here we can speak of urban spatial transformations, and a crucial development influencing the proliferation of "alternative" imagination—the multiplex, bearing what is often called a "multiplex film".

Hindi mainstream cinema of the 1990s, well exemplified by the emergence of young film-makers, such as Aditya Chopra and Karan Johar, was the cinema of euphoria—youth, luxury, global spaces, as well as submission to patriarchic authority are the dominant chronotopes. Such euphoric imagination can be contextualized keeping in mind the increasing presence of global commodities, rising affluence mainly in urban areas and among certain groups with access to global capital, global media flows and hybridized "glocal" ones through satellite television.

In parallel to the fascination with globalization and nationalism in mainstream cinema, there was another cinematic story—far darker, far more brutal and usually associated with the films of Ram Gopal Varma, focusing on the urban underbelly, a story that greatly influenced film-makers like Anurag Kashyap, to whom I will return later in the book

(Gopalan 2015). The 1990s, a decade following market reforms and the rise of Hindu nationalism, saw the emergence of film noir, a film form that is at the center of cinematic developments in the early 21st century. However, the first attempts at imagining a dark late-20th-century Indian metropolis (usually Mumbai) lacked the essential critical charge of neo-noir that was to appear later—a preoccupation with the critique of masculine insecurity. First experiments in noir can be seen as more organic articulations of changing perceptions of the city in the popular imagination despite the fact that the gangster films in question were self-conscious experiments very much influenced by global proliferation of noir esthetics roughly at the same time.

The Rise and Fall (and Rise) of Unhappy Consciousness

Anxiety, anger and frustration are marking the cultural landscape of the early 21st century in the times of increased marketization of life, political conservatism, nationalism and chauvinism and of the rise of global precariat. Such anxieties are by no means new, and can be seen as periodically emerging in the times of social changes, whatever those changes may be and wherever they may be occurring. Looking at this through the lens of cinema, as I shall do in this book, one can see the occurrences of anxiety and frustration in film noir, in neo-noir and in various film forms that have been influenced by these cinematic imaginations. Anxiety and frustration, neurotic and nihilistic imaginings and dark landscapes and psychoscapes, although traceable to the philosophical pessimism of the late 19th century, especially to Friedrich Nietzsche, speak of an ambivalent dialogue between the happy and unhappy consciousness in the age of neoliberal capitalism to me. Following the Frankfurt School, especially Herbert Marcuse we can look at manifestations of happy consciousness as affirmations of cultural status quo in society, or as ideologically invested objects of mass culture, to which most of Bollywood production belongs. Unhappiness, or what I am inclined to refer to as cinema of anxiety is the interrogative, sometimes critical representation of everyday life, culture, politics and society. In this book, in addressing differen aspects of darkness, I shall attempt to rethink the rise of cinematic anxiety and what can be cautiously perceived as unhappy consciousness. At the same time, the fall of unhappy consciousness and the rise of one-dimensionality can be understood in the deterioration of our perceptual apparatus and the flattening out of distinct dimensions that marked what we can call a modern period. Anxiety and imagining anxiety are the results of dromological shifts in contemporary culture: speed produces anxiety and atrophies the ability to generate organic unhappiness. Unhappy consciousness of today is in large part a mass-produced object masking the true origins of contemporary ennui. The problems in understanding and conceptually defining cinematic culture in the early 21st-century Hindi cinema, in my view, lie at the ambivalent crossroads of happiness and anxiety, mass-produced image and the work of art, critical thought and passive submission to the forces of the market.

For Marcuse, life has been sharply divided between sublimated high art and brutal reality, or material culture since time immemorial, and in the late 20th century, such division, making possible critical perspectives on life and world in the artistic and intellectual realm, is disappearing. According to Marcuse (2002: 64–5), art "unmasks reality, shows its mutilated content, its falsehood, exposes illusions". Art constructs a different reality, or a different space, where the discourse can be seen for what it really is, not for what it pretends to be, not as a myth it is forging about itself. Or, to put it differently, what is seen in a work of art is in tension with reality. Such tension between reality and art, and art's function in unmasking the reality by showing its real face may occupy the narrative of social change and emancipation. The lack of tension, or disappearance of it, produces a one-dimensional thought where critique is impossible.

We perhaps can see the manifestations of such overlapping between art and life with the rise of cinematic realism, primarily in post-War Italy, where film critics argued for erasing the dividing line between art and life. At the same time, the artistic sublimation of life, that is, in films of Roberto Rossellini and Vittorio De Sica, made possible precisely the unhappiness that is disappearing today. What is happening today in cinema globally is the reinvention of unhappy consciousness within the system, transformation and transmogrification that makes it difficult to distinguish between unhappy consciousness and manufactured dissenting imaginary. Such ambiguity in the age of neoliberal capitalism makes it extremely difficult and unproductive to see the cinematic universe as still subdivided into the conventional forms of yesteryear.

In Indian cinemas, the rise of cinematic unhappy consciousness began in the 1970s, during one of the most tumultuous periods in postcolonial India's history, with the emergence of the "Indian New Wave" as the first cinematic manifestation of it, which began with films like *Bhuvan Shome* (Mrinal Sen, 1969), *Sara Akash* (Basu Chatterjee, 1969), and *Uski Roti* (Mani Kaul, 1970). Later in the 1970s, during the height of social and political unrest following the rise of Naxalism in West Bengal and Indira Gandhi's Emergency, the new cinematic movement saw its momentum. From the sharp Marxist critiques of Ritwik Ghatak and Mrinal Sen in Bengali cinema, to the emergence of different and critical Hindi cinema esthetics of Shyam Benegal and, later, Govind Nihalani and Saeed Akhtar Mirza to the "middle cinema" of Basu Chatterjee and Hrishikesh Mukherjee—cinemas in India began to transform responding to the shifting social, political and cultural situation. Mainstream Hindi cinema, which in the post-liberalization period came to be known as Bollywood, also responded to the transforming landscape with much bleaker and violent urban visions, often in the form of a lone man, frustrated and fighting the system, embodied by Amitabh Bachchan's "angry young man" persona in films like *Zanjeer* or *Deewar*. Thus, the cinematic anxiety was the outcome of social, political and cultural anxieties in the post-Nehruvian period when a belief in developmentalist ideology declined and a postcolonial pessimism set in, producing disenchantment with the state and disillusionment with the developments in post-Independence India. The 1970s can be seen as a time when the cinematic unhappy consciousness was born.

In the 1980s, the New Wave began to wane due to the state's shifting focus from socially committed cinema to television. As mentioned before, this was also the time of rising political tensions, the emergence of radical nationalism that fed on the urban anxieties of the rising upper-caste middle classes. The New Wave never recovered, and was, until the period discussed in this book, limited to sporadic films catering to intellectual audiences. It is important to note that the rise of neoliberal capitalism in India and the marketization of life gave rise to a different type of cinematic unhappy consciousness as a means to channel out the anxiety. In an ambivalent move, neoliberal capitalism has been very successful in, on one hand, projecting its image of reality as the ultimate reality, where the reality represented is the image created by the discourse, and in flattening out the break between social reality and high culture, and on the other, facilitating the emergence of what is often perceived as alternative or critical cultural position. As Marcuse (2002: 60) states:

> Today's novel feature is the flattening out of the antagonism between culture and social reality through the obliteration of the oppositional, alien and transcendent elements in the higher culture by virtue of which it constituted *another dimension* of reality. This liquidation of *two-dimensional* culture takes place not through the denial and rejection of the "cultural values", but through their wholesale incorporation into the established order, through their reproduction and display on the massive scale.

Herein lies the biggest problem. The alternative, or unhappiness, is incorporated into a system and survives, indeed flourishes, as a commodified difference in one-dimensional space. What is left is a powerful feeling that multidimensional culture exists. Thus, the reproduction here means the reproduction of the discourse of neoliberalism on a mass scale and the interpellation of the subject to accept such one-dimensional culture as the ultimate one in a positive, unquestioning manner. The alternative culture transforms and merges with the dominant, one-dimensional culture as its variant—a more edgy, more fashionable one—but ultimately, a part of the same discourse, not a counter-cultural one. What was a counter-culture, a negative thinking, another dimension of reality, becomes a consumer product and is produced according to market-oriented values. It is necessary, therefore, that all alternatives are restructured in such manner that they lose their negativity. Also, the world has to be constructed as unproblematic, uncomplicated and unambiguous. Such ideology must make sure that no alternatives to its oppressive mechanisms could be articulated. Such acceptance that the world is unproblematic is, indeed, global. In this sense, neoliberal globalization is very effective. The sphere of the arts, which, in the words of Marcuse (2002), has been for long "another dimension" of reality—a dimension interrogating reality—has undergone massive change. Global economic changes in the 1980s and 1990s have pushed the latter problems even further. Neoliberalism proved to be very effective in producing "happy consciousness" on a mass scale, and at the same time, commodifying many spheres of life more intensely than any discourse, any ideology ever before. When things, ideas and feelings become commodities, the resistance against an oppressive system can itself become a commodity. The outcome of these processes—commodification of alternative, dissenting thought, where critique, rebellion, even revolution can become products to be sold and consumed. In this way, dissent is pacified before it even takes its form as such. It becomes fashionable to be alternative, to be *different*. Only that it has the appearance of one; it pretends to be alternative to the mainstream while instead projecting the present reality as unchanging, as given, as desired. In this way, what pretends to be a critique *becomes* a critique for those who consume it. In this way, a truly radical critique capable of addressing the problems of reality becomes marginalized, invisible and voiceless. Being an artist is difficult in a desublimated society where art and culture have become commodities, and the artist only has a function as a simple manufacturer of a product which, to be sure, must be unambiguous and unproblematic. Such a product cannot offer alternatives to the existing state of affairs, but surely, it can pretend to be doing so. In the end, the alternative presented can be the system itself—a negation of the very idea of alternative, but that is exactly the point of such production. In such a society, cinema finds it hard to re-complicate problems; it estheticizes them, but never deconstructs them. One may call the esthetic of this cinema a rebellious one, where not what the film shows, but how it shows it is very different. It may signify a development toward a different kind of perception and a new type of critique that is yet to emerge, but form without content does not make a work of art negative or "unhappy". The transformations in Hindi cinema in the age of neoliberalism can be understood as a rhizomatic flow and as a capital-led collapse of binaries in order to accommodate the alternative in the mainstream, thereby manufacturing one dimensionality. I am not privileging one approach over the other. I think both are valid. I think both processes are occurring simultaneously as the cultural transformations cannot be completely contained within the rigid logic of the market.

The New Wave can be seen as such organic art functioning in a two-dimensional space, and the emergence of new Hindi cinema in the early 21st century, as a transformed cultural difference, but only as a pastiche, in the words of Fredric Jameson (1991): "parody, the imitation of a peculiar or unique, idiosyncratic style, the wearing of a linguistic mask, speech in a dead language". He concludes, somewhat dreadfully, that "pastiche is thus blank parody, a statue with blind eyeballs" (Jameson 1991: 17). In his work on postmodernism, Jameson discusses several different paintings depicting the same object, shoes (Jameson 1991: 7–10), namely, Vincent Van Gogh's depiction of peasant shoes in *A Pair of Boots* (1886) and Andy Warhol's *Diamond Dust Shoes* (1980), outlining the mutation that occurred between the creation of both works, in order to illustrate his argument of transition to postmodern age. According to him, Warhol's work "turns centrally on commodification" (Jameson 1991: 9). While Van Gogh's shoes depict raw conditions, the reality itself—one can see the peasant's toil, the misery of life—Warhol's shoes are delicate, shiny, diamond-like that signify one thing, so central to our postmodern age or postmodern condition: fixation on depthlessness, on form without content and on the esthetization of everyday life. Life that is overwhelmed with images, that is mediated, that is more about style than substance. David Harvey in his discussion on Jameson talks of what the latter has called the depthlessness, and states that "Jameson has been particularly emphatic as to the 'depthlessness' of much of contemporary cultural production, its fixation with appearances, surfaces, and instant impacts that have no sustaining power over time" (Harvey 1990: 58). The talk here is about a move toward postmodernism in Western culture, a one-dimension-ality that perhaps unconsciously worried the scholars of the Frankfurt School before the actual advent of postmodernism. In the face of mass consumption and commodification where reality transforms into simu-lacra, where the push toward consumption as a greater good has been producing individuals and not citizens, not even societies, but simply clusters of consumers dwelling in the same space, is there anything that can counter-balance such tendencies? Is the counter-balance or negative thought even possible to contemplate?

Transition toward postmodernism or "liquid modernity" has been slowly brewing in India since the economic deregulation of the early 1990s, and transformation toward such a society, a hyper-industrial society of consumers, can be observed in full swing in the early 21st century. Is there any space left, one may ask, for negativity, unhappiness of thought, in such a space where almost anything can be transformed into a commodity? Negativity, dissent, critical thought and critical art are transforming into what Jameson (1991) terms "pastiche".

One can draw parallels between what occurred in the so-called "Western" culture when it moved toward postmodernism—while Van Gogh produced a work of art addressing the conditions of life, Warhol, in a different context and in a different age, reproduced it as a form without content. Similar parallels can be drawn in cinematic produc-tion—while Shyam Benegal or Govind Nihalani could be seen as pro-ducers of art addressing and interrogating reality, Anurag Kashyap or Vishal Bhardwaj reproduce products for consumption that are as shiny and stylish as Warhol's diamond shoes. It may signify a development toward a different kind of perception and a new type of critique that is yet to emerge, but as mentioned before, the negativity or "unhappiness" of such work of art is questionable It is for us to decide whether we choose to call such pastiche indie cinema.

Shanghai and *Matru ki Bijlee ka Mandola*

The mass reproduction of film forms seemingly penetrating into the uneasy tensions in 21st-century urban India's psyche means that the images that we can recognize as critical or dissenting and, at the same time, belonging to "art cinema" or "indie" reach us transformed and with their meaning changed, or in other words, we are witnessing a reification of culture in the times of neoliberal capitalism in India. Let's take *Shanghai* (Dibakar Banerjee, 2012) and *Matru ki Bijlee ka Mandola* (Vishal Bhardwaj, 2013) as examples. Both films are part of the new cinematic developments in Hindi cinema. The latter cannot be classified as "art cinema", if we look at it conventionally; it is entirely a commercial Bollywood product, and the former strongly flirts with art cinema both in terms of form and content.

Shanghai is a deeply political film, one can even say, a film committed to social change and critique of the previously mentioned status quo. But simultaneously, the film engages in a double move that works against such critique, thereby neutralizing it, or in other words, making the critique lose its negativity. The film therefore can be seen as balancing on the borderline, at the point when the positive absorbs the negative, but not yet fully. One can see the problematic negotiation and interplay between a desire for social change and an almost unconscious incapability to negotiate the alternative outside the system. *Shanghai's* main idea is the critique of developmental politics in rural India. The film takes place in the fictional town of Bharatnagar, in the middle of nowhere both literally and metaphorically, as the town exists only in the director's fantasy but can be recognized as any town in India. The town is waiting for a massive investment that would change it for the good and the construction of India Business Park—a massive Free Economic Zone project that would house a variety of business companies—would change it for the better. The project is referred to as the essence of progress and development, something that would turn the dusty and dirty middle-of-nowhere town into a new Shanghai. The project needs land that belongs to local peasants. The government and the corporations therefore try to dispossess the people of their land. The leader of resistance to this is Dr Ahmedi (Prosenjit Chatterjee), an NRI professor living in New York, who is projected as an epitome of leftist resistance to neoliberal conquests. He arrives at Bharatnagar in order to address a public gathering and speak against neoliberal development, but is

critically injured by a speeding truck shortly afterwards. The rest of
the film is an inquiry into his death—led by a state bureaucrat T.A.
Krishnan (Abhay Deol)—into who ordered it and who executed it.
Surely, everything points toward the highest political echelons and the
chief minister herself.

On the outside, the film seems to be a critique of the present state
of affairs in India, of developmental ideology, dispossession, poverty
and political cynicism. It may seem that the film agitates to rise against
corruption and stand with the "common man". It may seem that the
film is somewhat similar to the critical films made in the 1970s and
early 1980s that focused on rural, deprived India. However, this is not
the case. There are several problems with this film, and looking at each
one of them more closely may help us understand the nature of cultural politics in neoliberal India, the narratives and the images that are
produced in such milieu.

While it may seem that the film produces a critique of a market-
driven development administered by corrupt politicians without
exonerating the system that makes it possible, things are a bit more
complicated. Here, Banerjee does not cut through the reality in order
to show it for what it is. The unmasking and uncovering of "mutilated
content" of reality in the film is performed by a state bureaucrat, who is
part of the system, and by an NRI professor. These two are the ones with
whom the urban upper-middle-class audiences could identify easily, and
on top of that, in the end, it is the system itself that solves the problem;
the corruption, the murderous and inhuman face of development are
all exposed by the system's loyal servant, who dissents at the end of
the film. This is a misleading message, because it exonerates the system
itself—the system is good and well-functioning, but some reckless elements (read local state-level politicians) must be policed and disciplined.
It is the system that is the winner of the film and that eventually stands
by the "common man". In the end, we are glad that the system has such
moral servants: they prove that the system is good per se, only that it
needs some cleaning up to be done. In the end, we love the system and
are not inclined to rise against it. This is Orwellian thinking, and precisely in this type of thinking, all the potential negativity dissolves. This

is what Marcuse (2002) calls "the happy marriage of positive and the negative": it produces objective ambiguity and a false realism. Negative critique strives to uncover the irrational character of the system; it seeks to comprehend the root causes of rationality in order to transform it. However, this is not the case with *Shanghai*. The root causes are left barely touched, and the system that makes such reality possible is exonerated: it is not the system, but a few corrupt politicians that are at the heart of the problem. The film provides critical insights with regards to the relationship of business and politics, with regards to dissent and the need to unmask the mutilated content of politics, but at the same time, the space it produces is enchanted and exotified. Bharatnagar is an unreal place, a non-place that does and does not exist, and where the urban middle class and the outsiders, in a more general sense, can wage imaginary battles for the poor and the dispossessed.

In a very similar fashion, such an imaginary space that arouses the imagination, quenches the potential for dissent and participates in the "marriage of positive and negative" is recreated in another fictional town, Mandola, in *Matru ki Bijlee ka Mandola*. The film's theme itself addresses a serious and important topic as *Shanghai* does—development not for the sake of the people, but for the sake of a few select individuals who would profit from it. It is a dark comedy, set in a small town which once again encounters brutal developmentalism for the benefit of the political elite and the corporations. The town is ruled over by a local landlord Harry Mandola. He and the state's chief minister desire to develop the town by taking over the land belonging to the peasants, and building factories, shopping malls and housing complexes on it. The peasants are organized and resist. The leader of the resistance, whose identity is disclosed only later in the film, is a mysterious quasi-Naxalite curiously known only by the nickname Mao. Mandola the landlord is a drunkard and suffers from what can be termed as a personality disorder: when he is drunk, he is a cheerful person, is with the peasants and supports their cause. But when he is sober, he is a brutal landlord and he constantly moves between the two states of mind. In one scene at the beginning of the film, while drunk, he leads a popular revolution against the landlord (that is, against himself) and marches toward the landlord's mansion (his own). Accidentally, he falls into a swimming pool while doing this, sobers up and realizes to his horror that he had led a revolution against himself. This duality between revolt and conformity, as if between happy and unhappy consciousness, is an interesting one; it asks questions about the limits of dissent, possibilities of revolt, but ultimately, it works against all possible negativity, and once again produces a happy consciousness. In the end, the evil chief minister gets what she deserves, and it is again the system itself, in the form of Mandola, that solves the problem or corrects itself—not the masses, not the revolution, but the elite and the system solve the problem. And we, the spectators, as the peasants in the film, love Mandola (or the system) for what he/it has accomplished.

The message received from the films is an ambiguous one: one can revolt and support the revolt only in the state of drunken delirium. But one has to sober up sooner or later and wake up to the reality which is always more complex than it seems when you are drunk. The landlord, the evil oppressor, proves to be not so evil after all and understands his mistakes. In the end, the chief revolutionary Mao marries Mandola's daughter. While Banerjee's Bharatnagar is a dark and eerie, indeed, dystopic place, the town of Mandola is not—it is fetishized to be a fun place, a place of festival, drunkenness, revolt, brave farmers, evil landlords, a place fun to visit, fun to peek into.

The two films I discussed provide us with a feeling of alternative and can be seen as a form without content or a form with drastically transformed content, which is no longer graspable if we choose to look at it conventionally. Benegal's *Ankur* (1974) and *Nishant* (1975), both set in rural India, articulated dissatisfaction with social and political conditions and perhaps could be seen as representing the subaltern or attempting to speak for them. Such attempts are there in *Shanghai* and *Matru ki Bijlee ka Mandola*, but function as commodities.

It is hard not to agree with Zygmunt Bauman's (2000: 48) skepticism about the prospects of critical discourse, as it was formulated by some of the Frankfurt School theorists, especially Adorno, in the postmodern age or in "liquid modernity" as he calls it . According to him, the critical theory of that time in the present moment is losing its subject. Critique transforms according to the changing times, the same way consumption of certain images disrupts the critique. Society, and modernity per se, with tendencies toward totalitarianism and a closely guarded, surveilled, one-dimensional society, is giving way to something new, something raw and yet to be fully comprehended—an individualistic society that functions as a market, according to market-oriented values. Such a society made up of consumer-individuals not only finds it hard to re-complicate the problems and produce a critique, but also the very idea of critique in such a society is not on the agenda. Postmodern, neoliberal discourse produces *a society without a society*, if one may use such a notion, made up squarely of individuals as atoms, as consumers. Stiegler (2011: 6–7) talks of a "hyper-industrial" society and states that consumer society replaces a democratic one. What emerge in the process, according to him, are different forms of social organization and the consumer society. For him, this signifies decadence of society. His ideas are similar to Bauman's and Jameson's when it comes to transformations toward postmodern or liquid states of existence and experience. According to Stiegler (2014: 6–7), "since the appearance of the industrial technologies of sound and image that made them possible, the culture industries have become organs capable of creating identification processes via behavioural models, which are themselves incessantly renewed according to the demands of innovation". Precisely this renewal can be observed in Indian cinemas that correspond to the changing demands of the public, of the new urban middle class. What emerges is the differentiated product that creates and reflects new forms of identification. This identification, and what it stands for, represents the needs of a new India and the new consumers—consumers that are interpellated by the new culture industries as "happy".

Therefore, thought in such a society is no longer even one-dimensional: it is dislocated to such an extent that talking about dimensions might be problematic—there are simply too many of them. Would it be possible to call such a society—which, let us provisionally state, is no longer a society—an *un-dimensional* one? Are empathy, affect and care even possible? Could negativity and unhappiness be parts of the postmodern discourse? One must remember the unhappiness and existential angst of Anant (Om Puri) in *Ardh Satya* (Govind Nihalani, 1983). A hardened and honest police officer, Anant reads a poem that changes his life. The poem in the film (a work of art *inside* the work of art) re-complicates, and indeed dislocates, the character and makes him reflect on his life as a policeman functioning in a system that is corrupt and rotten, and by extension makes him reflect upon the futility of being honest in a society where such values are not appreciated. It makes him realize that something is not right, both inside the society and inside his soul. Similar inner tension and dissatisfaction is expressed in other films of that time, and ironically, can anyone be more direct than Saeed Akhtar Mirza by asking the question very bluntly in the title of one of his films—*Albert Pinto Ko Gussa Kyon Ata Hai?* (1980). Why is the individual, a hard-working mechanic Albert Pinto (Naseeruddin Shah) who dreams of affluence, unhappy? At the same time, those who watch the film and grasp the message may start reflecting on the problems in the society and perhaps begin to ask similar questions.

In short, if we compare thematically similar films of these two distinct periods, we can see instances of cultural reification occurring in the neoliberal period. But how should we as philosophers and film scholars understand the present cultural reification, the crystallization of esthetic difference, variously referred to as indie, New Bollywood, hatke, middlebrow—a form that cannot be easily categorized (it can be called a new genre, a new form, new style, a phenomenon and so on)? The different cinema, whatever term we as scholars may give it, is the result of the collapse of rigid binary oppositions, a boundary demarcating what was once known as Bollywood and indie cinema. Of course, mainstream Bollywood and indie have not disappeared; what emerged in the in-between space was an undecideable space, to use Derrida's term, which began to produce new meanings and new interpretations of transforming India under neoliberalism. There may be different ways to theorize this "twilight" zone, which makes an esthetic communication between the mainstream and "art" an actuality, as debates surrounding the emergent newness clearly portray. I think the desire to categorize the emergent newness, to pin it down and compartmentalize it on a highly unstable cultural terrain, to give a "name" to newness, are problematic occurrences in academic acrobatics rooted in the structural clarities of the modern age. Naming is more important for us, scholars and film critics, as an analytical category, while the reality of cultural flux far too often escapes us. Cinematic transformations occurring today are necessarily rhizomatic; it is a deterritorialized flow of form (Deleuze and Guattari 2004: 260–94) cutting across different genres in Hindi cinema. Deleuze and Guattari (2013: 26), explaining what they mean by a rhizome, offer the following description: "A rhizome has no beginning or end; it is always in the middle, between things, interbeing, intermezzo". Extending their argument, they state that: "*Between* things does not designate a localizable relation going from one thing to the other and back again, but a perpendicular direction, a transversal movement that sweeps one *and* the other away, a stream without beginning or end that undermines its banks and picks up speed in the middle" (Deleuze and Guattari 2013: 27).

Unexpected cultural formations—impossible to categorize or indeed influence—mark such spontaneous rhizomatic movements. The fluidity of film form and free incorporation of different esthetic elements throughout the Hindi cinema, be it mainstream or not, is symptomatic. Rhizome defies control, be it a cultural–creative control, political control or an academic one, in the process of producing theory accounting for this cinematic phenomenon. But one should also celebrate such freedom and openness cautiously, because it just as well may be simulacra. It is important to note that the free-flowing form functions within capitalist economy is a product of it and is bound to it. This flow is not a threat to the dominant esthetics of consumerist culture, but is a symptom of adaptation to transformed social landscape and media environment. Cinematic transformations are symptoms of neoliberal tremors that have been slowly refiguring life itself, giving birth to new sociocultural sensibilities as well as new social class formations.

2

OBJECTS IN THE MIRROR ARE CLOSER THAN THEY APPEAR
Imagination and the Other

In one of the most important scenes in *NH10*—outside Gurgaon (now Gurugram), in the brutal wilderness of Haryana's Other India—the film's protagonists Meera and Arjun are traveling in their SUV and lose their way. Arjun stops the car at a roadside dhaba to ask for directions. As he walks over to the men sitting there, Meera stays alone in the car. She sits on the passenger seat. All of a sudden, a man, a local villager, appears next to the side window and asks if they were looking for the road to Basantpura, which they were. Meera does not say anything; she looks scared and rolls up the side window. Arjun comes back to the car and they drive off slowly. Meera looks in the rear-view mirror and sees the man looking at her. The mirror, like all rear-view mirrors of the motor vehicles in India, states: "Objects in the Mirror Are Closer Than They Appear." The scene is very brief and despite the drama that unfolds later in the film, the reflection of the Other leaves an imprint in the unconscious. Meera looks at the Other's reflection with fear and disgust. Indeed, as we learn later in the film, the Other is much closer than it appears—much closer than Meera and Arjun, an upper-middle-class couple having corporate jobs and living in a cozy luxury apartment in Gurgaon, may wish.

NH10 works through the dichotomy of self and Other and makes use of spaces that are outside the dreamy lifeworlds of neoliberal or global India. By outside, I mean the material spaces geographically outside the major metropolitan areas—small towns and villages that, in relation to the 21st-century city, are located in another time, in another space. The Other and the Other space of the emergent class are knowable and physically close but, mentally, are far removed and the knowledge of the Other resides in the unconscious. Such spaces are created in relation to other spaces and are heterotopian emplacements or place-images. In the case of urban India, they are forged in the process of urban transformation, and marginal because they are placed on the margins for a purpose. Such (em)placement, such relevance of the Other for the construction of the self is one of the psychoanalytical objects of inquiry. However, in visual culture and in the process of mass mediation, the importance of the Other as a symbol of what the emergent self is not migrates from the unconscious into popular culture and this "dark side" of new urban India's self in the making is more evident than before. Films that depart from the city but clearly remain within the city in casting their gaze at the peripheries form an important part of new Hindi cinema. If films focusing on transforming lives in the cities could be seen as examples of imagining the self, the films focusing on small-town India or Other India imagine, to some extent, the lives of the Other, but more importantly, the relation of urban self and the peripheric Other. I would call the trend of many films to drift away from the dominance of urban center as the center of imagination *a desire for the Other*. This desire could be two-fold: it is a desire for Other India—peripheral, unruly, marginal in terms of what are the target audiences of such films. A desire for the Other is also a more mundane desire for other esthetics, a desire for difference and a differentiated cultural product. So, the difference in this case also presents us with multiplicity.

Otherness and Neoliberal Imagination

Peripheral spaces of the Other in many films representing rural or small-town India function as unreal or semi-real places. Their function is to provide a space, the Other space of the Other India, against which the neoliberal and largely urban India could negotiate its self. In addition to positing a positive thinking and reducing any potential for dissent, these films forge a duality of self and Other by encoding spaces with unreal, magical and exciting qualities. I would call these semi-real spaces neoliberal heterotopia. *NH10* also projects trajectories of movement or navigation in neoliberal space—the film refers to a highway leading further away from the comforts of upper-class dwellings in Delhi. New Hindi cinema's imaginary journeys, therefore, are "the prostheses of accelerated voyages", as Virilio (2009: 71) describes the phenomenon. We need the slum-dweller, as without one, we would not know *what to become.* As Stiegler (2014: 32) puts it, "it is a time about which we do not know what we should think" as the hyper-industrial epoch is a time of misery, because we do not know what we should be or how the market helps us. Also in the case of the new upper classes in urban India, cinematic journeys into a different space are a commodified answer to such existential disorientation of the emerging neoliberal human being. The market produces peculiar brands through which we can singularize. The films in question therefore transition toward post-cinematic form in becoming thingified. In this sense, films become tools that we can make use of for constructing the self.

The so-called "newness" or reification, whether we speak of developments in Hindi cinema or of any new "cutting edge" cultural developments, is itself a problematic category. Boris Groys (2014: 3) argues that "the peculiarity of the concept of the new prevalent in the modern period resides, after all, in the expectation that, eventually, something so definitively new will emerge that there can never be anything still newer thereafter". He further states that "the desire for the new is the desire for truth" (Groys 2014: 9). Capitalism historically strives for newness in all spheres of life, for the evaporation of solidity (Berman 2010). Neoliberalism accelerates such desire for the new and the speed of transforming relationships to the phenomena is ever stronger. The desire of the new may be the desire for truth, but what happens to the psyche of the "new" neoliberal subject when the emergence of newness is integral to the process of acceleration—both in terms of economic, sociocultural transformations and in terms of vision? What does this do to the perception of self and Other, as well as of material environment? Is it not the disappearance, instability and ephemerality we should be talking about, as Virilio does? Emergent newness in the form of new artistic forms of expression must be critically evaluated, especially speaking of such media as cinema, given the extreme nature of commodification under neoliberalism.

Newness can be and always should be interrogated, as it has all the potential of being one of the sources of happy consciousness. In neoliberal times, newness and innovation are far too often celebrated as indications of entrepreneurial qualities of *homo oeconomicus*—qualities that are valorized more than any others. Emergence of new alternatives and innovations are loudly greeted in a vast array of circles—among consumers, critics and in the media. As if the alternative to mainstream culture is indeed a schizophrenic movement disrupting the limits of capitalism, as if alternative and seemingly independent cultural work by its mere existence confirms that not everything belongs within the discourse of neoliberal capitalism (Deleuze and Guattari 2004). As Mark Fisher (2009: 9) claims, "'alternative' and 'independent' don't designate something outside mainstream culture; rather, they are style, in fact the dominant styles, within the mainstream". Deleuze and Guattari (2004, 2013) have explored the depths and problems of capitalism and possibilities and impossibilities of subversive, nomadic flows and rhizomatic formations. According to them, the capitalist system or capitalist discourse has two limits—internal and external—and they call the latter a schizophrenic limit, or we may say, the ultimate subversive alternative crossing the boundary of alternative or independent art that functions as a necessary part of neoliberal discourse. According to Deleuze and Guattari (2004), capitalism perpetually displaces its limits so they could never be reached. When "alternative" moves outside of what is acceptable, capitalism pushes the limit, incorporating such subversion as part of its own discourse. A system or discourse must have oppositional elements functioning within itself if it wants to continue functioning without major disruptions. But these elements never question the system—they function to affirm it. We may call this quasi-oppositional element a *difference*. This difference must exist in order to act as an affirmation of the system's self. In time, of course, new differences emerge; small particles are born like small cracks in the system, but as soon as they are born, they get reterritorialized as integral part of the system. One never knows how or when or in what form such difference or newness might emerge, but one thing is certain: it would never be left to live a life of its own, it would never be allowed to function in a rhizomatic existence. The birth of difference or new-ness or counter-culture is both needed and expected. As Deleuze and Guattari (2004: 272) say, in the voice of the system, "we'll always find a place for you within the expanded limits of the system, even if the axiom has to be created just for you". Furthermore, they say that the system "has a peculiar passion for such things that leaves the essential unchanged" (Deleuze and Guattari 2004: 275). I propose to locate the emergent esthetics as precisely such newness or difference—a peculiar-ity a system has a passion for, but difference that is allowed to exist only because it has already been reterritorialized as an internal part of the system at the exact moment of its birth. There is, of course, a theoreti-cal possibility of breaking out, of an element that the system fails to capture in its net, that it fails to reterritorialize. Such a particle can fly all the way to reach the external limit, which Deleuze and Guattari (2004) call the schizophrenic limit. In a crucial passage, they make the following statement, which is central in understanding the current situation in "alternative" cinema, which is hardly alternative to anything besides stylistic transfigurations:

> Schizophrenia, on the contrary, is indeed the absolute limit that causes the flows to travel in a free state.... Hence one can say that schizo-phrenia is the exterior limit of capitalism itself or the conclusion of its deepest tendency, but that capitalism only functions on condition that it inhibit this tendency, or that it push back or displace the limit, by substituting for its own immanent relative limits, which it continually reproduces on a widened scale. (Deleuze and Guattari 2004: 267)

The present discourse of neoliberal India needs such "alternative" or "indie" styles, spaces, semi-real places and the dispossessed that no lon-ger come to haunt the privileged by their mere presence because "the poor are no longer at the gates; bosses live in enclaved communities a world away, beyond political or legal reach. Capital and its workforce become more and more remote from each other. Here is the harsh underside of the culture of neoliberalism" (Comaroff and Comaroff 2001: 13).

Another crucial element in the transformed cinematic landscape is the constant presence of the Other in its many forms. In the most obvious instance, the Other can be seen as the village juxtaposed to the city, poverty as opposed to affluence and subalternity as opposed to hegemony. A number of scholars have pointed out the centrality of a village in the context of Indian imagination, both in terms of a cinematic one and more broadly as part of Indian modernity. Many have emphasized that a village as an idea has played an important part in imagining the urban life (Inden 2001; Nandy 2007). Sanjay Srivastava (2014: 95) relates the colonial romanticism, commodification of it in neoliberal India and transformation of the idea of a village into a commodity—spaces where one can "experience 'authentic' rural food and entertainment" and wander in "purpose-built 'ethnic villages'". These are the actual spaces performing a function in subject formation. Such spaces are the Foucauldian heterotopias that I will speak about throughout the book. On the imaginary level, there are other imagined spaces that contribute in fueling the imagination of the middle class and the consolidation of feeling and belonging to the middle class and related sensibilities.

A prevalent trend that most of the new Bollywood films share is the focus on the dark side of city life—an urban uncanny, incorporating different elements of film noir form, like *Talaash* (Reema Kagti, 2012); Anurag Kashyap's work like *That Girl in Yellow Boots* (2010), *Ugly* (2013) and *Raman Raghav 2.0* (2016) or even Dibakar Banerjee's interpretation of a Bengali classic making it even more noir than the original, *Detective Byomkesh Bakshy!* (2015). Most of them in one form or the other have a threatening and disruptive otherness present as a crucial element. The film form of noir has had a tremendous impact on the new Hindi cinema, either consciously (as in the case of Anurag Kashyap) or unconsciously. In this book, I do not intend to focus on the technical aspects of film-making generally important in the analysis of

noir but will look at the films sociologically, at the social reality that
made the new imaginary possible. Here, indeed, one can observe a
general trend on the global scale: social transformations do cause the
emergence of nostalgia for the seemingly uncomplicated social relations of the past, fear for the present and paranoia for ephemeral age
of social change. This aspect, the dark imagination, is one of the key
problems analyzed in this book.

Many films do focus on the space that is peripheral to the class
they are aimed at—this space can be the urban underworld, uncanny
upper-middle-class space or a mofussil periphery. The films construct
what I would like to term the "Other India", but in any case, gazing
is performed from the metropolis and it is directed at the space in-
between, both real and imagined at the same time—a space we may
call heterotopian (Foucault 2000). Why do such *heterotopian spaces* of
small-town films appeal to those who have little to do with small towns
in real life? Prasad (2000: 67) in his influential book *Ideology of the
Hindi Film* states that:

> From the organic space of the north Indian village to the high-tech tour-
> ist spots of the world, the feudal structure demonstrates how powerful
> its ideological hold was and to an extent still is. This structure could
> incorporate consumerism and other "modern" features without damage
> as long as it did not slide into a position of affirmation of new sexual and
> social relations based on individualism. The "foreign" values that came in
> for vicious criticism occasionally were a code word for democracy and a
> capitalism based on the generalization of free labour.

The ideological tensions of the 1990s that Prasad analyzes in his
study—the mental journeys from "organic spaces of north Indian village" to the "high-tech tourist spots"; the unease about the modern,
the foreign, the sexual newness, objects of desire and desire infused
with dread—all this has transformed in the first two decades of the
21st century. Transformed, reterritorialized, but present nevertheless.
New social relations and the emergence of new subjectivities can be
viewed as a break from the "feudal family romance" that dominated
social imaginary as well as popular Hindi cinema for a very long time.

Consumerism and new hybrid cultural norms no longer have a need to negotiate the potential "damage" Prasad is talking about. Democracy, capitalism and neoliberal "foreign" cultural practices became an integral part of the new Indian middle class's emergent self. The new Indian middle class may be small compared to the massive sections of society outside the realm of "neoliberal dream-worlds", but the imaginary of this dominant class, its global and local visibility, as well as influence of its cultural codes as a dominant class produces an aspirational culture— a desire to become a part of this class, a desire to consume and internalize its cultural sensibilities.

Ashis Nandy has argued that cinema is a slum eye view of politics. He stated that "the popular cinema … is also the disowned self of modern India returning in a fantastic or monstrous form to haunt modern India" (Nandy 1998: 7). While the haunting may be far more complex nearly two decades after Nandy wrote these words, the main reason why his argument is no longer valid is the reversal of the object of desire. The fearsome Other does haunt what he calls modern India but it is a different India that is haunted, and haunted differently. A mofussil, a small town or a village as an idea is no longer a "pastoral 'paradise'" for the urban self he talked about (Nandy 1998: 5). Peripheries are no longer imaginary spaces of origin one desires, and translates that desire into cinematic form for, nor are there any needs for imaginary journeys to cities. Instead, we need imaginary journeys into the peripheries, but these are very different from the ones performed by Mrinal Sen, whose work Nandy (2007: 72–97) discusses. These are different imaginary journeys from the ones performed by Amitabh Bachchan in *Zanjeer* or *Deewar* (Mazumdar 2007: 1–41). A film is a dromoscope, to use Virilio's (2008) notion, a vessel: a "ship" functioning as a vehicle into the unconscious that helps us travel and, by doing so, forming our subjectivity. As Foucault (2000: 185) has said, "in civilizations without ships the dreams dry up". But such dreams can also be deeply disturbing ones, with neurotic imaginary of becoming-self bringing no solace, only fear, delirium and anxiety.

With accelerating speed and technological innovations, the reality transforms from a solid one into a liquid, to use Bauman's (2000) term.

With the rise of television, social networking, mobile technologies and Internet as platforms to disseminate submission to the capital, reality transforms into what can possibly be called a virtual reality or a virtual space that functions according to very different rules of gravity. It is very important to emphasize that such "liquidity" and immateriality in India almost exclusively belongs to the urban upper-middle class, which gets increasingly removed or isolated from the material reality outside its space. This class—the main benefactor of neoliberalism: the consumer and the producer of images about itself and an epitome of a "good life" ambiguously "casts disenchanted eye to the world", as Jacques Rancière (2009: 37) has put it. Simultaneously, it re-enchants the space outside in the fashion of a theme park, of exotic unreality. Akhil Gupta (2012: 21–2) in his work on structural violence rightly states:

> One must keep in mind that certain classes of people have a stake in perpetuating a social order in which such extreme suffering is not only tolerated but also taken as normal. All those who benefit from the status quo and do not want to see it changed then become complicit in this violence against the poor. In a country like India, the perpetrators of violence include not only the elites but also the fast-growing middle class, whose increasing number and greater consumer power are being celebrated by an aggressive global capitalism.

The films that can be seen as belonging to *alternative esthetics* of the present times are produced by and for this class, which celebrates itself and is celebrated as *global India*. Such an India, in addition to tolerating suffering, which Gupta (2012) refers to, and living in its microcosm of shopping malls, multiplexes and sports utility vehicles (SUVs), re-imagines or re-enchants the rest of India in such a manner that poverty becomes esthetically beautiful, even romantic. This class celebrates itself and its lifestyle probably less vigorously than before when it comes to the imagination, but casts its eye toward its Other, fetishizing it, perpetuating the status quo of inequality, but nevertheless need-ing it in order to have its new self consolidated. Neoliberal esthetics therefore sublimates crisis and compliments what Gupta (2012) calls a structural violence against the poor. Only that in the present case, this violence against the Other takes a form of representation; it becomes representational violence in order to satisfy the pleasure one gets from imagining otherness.

The process of cinematic transformations embedded in the neo-liberal cultural project coincided with overall media transformations, emergence of new media forms and new patterns of film consumption. The content of the films may often seem socially and politically relevant, at times addressing sensitive issues (for example, political corruption, developmental problems and various forms of violence and poverty). There might be an instinctive impulse to celebrate the emergence of newness, a more realistic one, which departs from the so-called escapist fantasies that dominated Hindi cinema earlier. However, before celebrating the newness of new Hindi cinema, we should stop for a while, as the newness offered by this genre and their representatives is far more complex than it might seem at first. Newness, innovation and cutting-edge developments in all spheres of life are some of the most exalted elements in the neoliberal value system. In arts, too, innovation, relentless transformation and transmogrification is valorized and celebrated. Steven Shaviro (2010: 45), drawing upon Gilles Deleuze's (2005) concept of any-space-whatever and its "unlimited possibilities" as space of "pure potential", claims that capitalism effectively exploits such possibilities and potential in commodifying such spaces and spheres of human activity in the form of "events, experience, moods, memories, hopes, and desires". Any form of art, indeed, any cultural activity is bound to be commodified and it is up to the producers of art and culture to negotiate their freedom, invention and the possibilities of critique within the commodified space. Transforming Hindi cinema in this case is wholly a product of the market appealing to and representing shifting sensibilities, quietly producing hopes and desires as needed by the market. However, though it is a differentiated product, it makes use of its *alternative* potential in representing the transforming space of the real world.

It is useful to analyze these problems in applying a spatial concept of heterotopia, introduced by Michel Foucault. According to him, heterotopia is an actually existing place—a place that is ambiguous: real, but simultaneously infused with imaginary qualities. In every society, any heterotopian emplacement has a function and functions in relation with real places. Heterotopia, therefore, is "actually realized utopia in which the real emplacements, all the other real emplacements that can be found within a culture are, at the same time, represented, contested, and reversed, sorts of places that are *outside* all places, although they are actually localizable" (Foucault 2000: 178, emphasis mine).

Such space, therefore, needs to be treated as localizable, while simultaneously *being outside*. A real space, which could be treated as being in a problematic relationship with reality itself. If a single screen of the yesteryear was an open space, the multiplex is an exclusive, closed space; it is a space constructed in order to tame the unruly masses, to civilize them or to initiate them into a civilized mode of consumption. It is a closed space because it filters out the unwanted elements—the poor, the subaltern if you will, the pavement dwellers. Just like at a shopping mall, one can consume in peace. Next to the mainstream masala, you always have what has come to be known as a multiplex film: a film or product specifically designed to be consumed only at a multiplex, by a certain crowd. Of course, such films can be consumed at home as well, on a plasma TV set, in the tranquility of one's living room. What is being projected is the space of the Other or other India in terms of who the main "receiver and consumer" of the film is.

Heterotopia, the way I use it, is a space produced by cinema: it is imaginary, but curiously resembles and *wants* to resemble real life. It is ambiguous: it is real but simultaneously infused with imaginary qualities. Any film can qualify for such a description. In every society, any heterotopian emplacement has a function, and functions in relation with real places. Cinema as a heterotopian space with all its neoliberal implications does complicate the picture, as the space is imagined on screen and is physically removed from a real place and transplanted in a multiplex. Cinema does make us travel to such a heterotopia, experience and consume difference, primitivism and violence by remaining spectators, without getting involved, safely in a comfortable seat of a cinema hall, because this is the life of the Other—not our life, always someone else's. By buying a ticket, we are sold a peculiar "holiday package tour" into a heterotopia of either primitive India, violent India or India in crisis. This constructed space is always someone else's India, which can be experienced, providing an illusion of living. Living elsewhere, and perhaps, in another time.

Heterotopia has a function in relation to the remaining space. In the present case, it creates a space of illusion that denounces all real space, but an illusion that is needed as the Other life, as the experience of the Other life. Consumption, therefore, in this case, is needed in order to constitute a self. In a neoliberal culture, consumption constitutes a neoliberal self. Imagination, power of images and the illusory nature of reality are all very important. "Shining India" therefore, in order to imagine itself, needs to re-enchant the rest of India and construct it as a kind of imaginary space. Indeed, it has to imagine it, and to feel, to experience through the medium of an image what it is like to dwell in that Other India, what it means to live a different life. In this way, dusty towns in the middle of nowhere and highways leading away from gated comfort zones become heterotopian spaces that can be consumed for the pleasure of it. Those who inhabit those spaces are semi-real people reduced to bare life. This fantasy is constructed for consumption and the reason for it is quite simple: it no longer corresponds to the reality of those who consume it. It is no longer painful; it no longer is something one would want to forget, to erase from memory as an embarrassment. At the same time, it is not a reality one would desire to change. It is convenient to have it, necessary indeed, for the postcolonial imaginary to unfold. This Other India is no longer a problem as such for those who consume these images. One can be alarmed about the absence of empathy in those who could affect change, but this absence is not surprising. Any care or empathy would stand in the way of consumption and reproduction of goods and images.

However, if noir imagination is a new phenomenon deeply related to the transforming cities in the late 20th century, the preoccupation with the Other and juxtapositions of urban self and rural Other are not, and have roots in colonial relationship between the colonizer and the colonized, in bourgeoisie—lower class dichotomies in the Marxian sense, and the perceptions of the city/center and the country/periphery (Williams

1973). An important example from pre-neoliberal India—which, in terms of trajectory "from city to rural wilderness" bears some similarities to *NH10* and to other films I shall discuss later—is the Bengali film *Aranyer Din Ratri* (Satyajit Ray, 1970). It sharply juxtaposes what can be termed as urban sophistication and rural "backwardness". In the film, four friends travel from Calcutta (now Kolkata) to rural West Bengal in what becomes an experience of otherness. They feel they are a part of a sophisticated middle class and can use the Other in every way they want, including sexual exploitation of local tribal women. "What a life!" exclaims Ashim (Soumitra Chatterjee), while drunk on local moonshine. In this scene, the four friends sit in a local bar, an outdoor shack, and the image of it is being juxtaposed with a memory image of a high-society party in Calcutta. What the urban characters in the film *do* can be understood as an experience of the other India, as well as a quasi-anthropological examination of otherness. John Frow (1997: 9) speaks of "non-synchronicity" and draws upon the anthropological work of Johannes Fabian, according to whom—from the perspective of an anthropologist—the people studied by this discipline occupy a different time, a time past. This is, of course, a much broader problem in representation that has been occupying postcolonial scholars for the past four decades. The one who studies or the one who has the power to represent and to speak for the Other occupies a different imaginary time than the one who is (mis)represented. This is similar to Foucault's notion. The represented one (or a represented subaltern) in the films mentioned earlier occupies a different time and space in such a representation, which is very different from art cinema's engagement with the same, though not without exceptions. I argue that such "non-synchronicity" is visible in imagining rural and unlawful India in recent films. This phenomenon signifies a widening gap between the urban rich and the poor, both urban and rural, and as Frow rightly states, the primary producer and consumer of this imagination is the urban middle class. The fact that this class does consume this, that it craves for it, feeds on it, thrives on the escape into the past India, displaced India, could mean spatial fragmentation between "Shining India" and "imagined India"—a break between different Indias with different purposes in the neoliberal discourse. This break then signifies a departure and emplacement of Other India as heterotopia, no longer real, still having a concrete place, but infused with unreal qualities. Such is the Other India in *Aranyer Din Ratri*. This break thus makes the construction of bare life, or even a *bare life of the image*, to paraphrase Giorgio Agamben (1998), possible.

These are the basic functions of the films and the spaces they imagine. First, the films produce positive thinking by blending different genres—mainstream cinema and art cinema—where the negative potential of the latter dissolves, where the real issues and inequalities become fetishized and the spectator-consumer is indoctrinated or interpellated to love the system, which has the power to correct itself. On a deeper level, or on a level of the filmic unconscious, the films enact a space of difference, which, by being a semi-real space or a heterotopia, evoke the spirit of a theme park, a fascinating, backward, primitive space populated by freaks who are unproblematic entertainers, and which can be a playground of the urban rich on the imaginary level, and on the level of social reality, a playground of those who strive to represent the subaltern, to fight for them or to deny any representation and dignity of life whatsoever. These two functions combined produce a bare life, an imaginary one, a cinematic one, which removes the spectator-consumer from any feelings of empathy. Commodification of heterotopia and encoding of this heterotopia as a space of difference that only has a function vis-à-vis the real India as its Other contributes toward the imagining of duality that is necessary for consolidating the global India's' self. This, then, both signifies the distance between classes and produces a space in which the classes not belonging to rising India can be consumed as a product, a piece of exotica for in-house consumption. It also makes lack of empathy possible, because those places are semi-real. All this signifies a departure of the urban middle class into its own other India, an imaginary global India that still retains a relationship with that really real India of the rest of the people, but the relationship is problematic.

On the one hand, one also has to consider those in whose name the battles are fought, those who dwell in the unreality of imaginary

Other space, and, on the other hand, in the suffocating reality of real emplacements before they are lifted up, constructed and imagined for consumption: the subaltern masses in rural India. I will not go deep into the questions of subalternity, but would like to make a point with regards to representation. This is related to the previous arguments on commodification and production of heterotopologies. The relationship between the consumer and "the consumed" resembles a classic relationship between the colonizer and the colonized, between the center and the periphery or production of the Orient for the West and by the West, as Edward Said (1978) has demonstrated. At the same time, it is possible to speak of a production of "postcolonial exotic" for the consumption—not by the West, but by the already departed urban upper-middle class. This functions internally inside the postcolonial space, which is split between "rising India" and India as a heterotopian commodity. The difference, therefore, as opposed to the evocations of the same, say, in the works of Ritwik Ghatak or Mrinal Sen, in addition to being desirable, is unproblematic in a sense that it does not try to re-complicate the matter of representation and does not try to combat the actual oppression on the political level.

The subalterns on screen have always been freaks evoking difference, but being a freak or being marginal could serve and would serve in the present as oppositional deconstructive quality with regards to the dominant ideology (in this case, neoliberal exploits in the peripheries). The films I discuss have no shortage of freaks. In the process of creating a heterotopian space, in the construction of subalternity as commodity, and the peripheral location as an imaginary holiday destination into another space and another time, freaks are deprived of the subversive potential. In experiencing the epistemic violence and reduction to bare life in the cinematic image, the freaks continue living but live transformed as the objects of fascination for what they are, because "they are no longer images of another way of life, but rather freaks of types of the same life, serving as an affirmation rather than negation of the established order" (Marcuse 2002: 59). Affirmation in this case means freak as a form without content, functioning in a space that has been converted into the other reality. In this other reality or other space, freaks/subalterns are entertainers for the urban, upper-middle-class spectators sitting in dimly lit cinema halls, engrossed in enjoyment of seductive otherness. At the same time, if we presuppose that the focus on subversive characters by filmmakers (for example, Dalits, urban poor, minorities, etc.) was for the urgency to represent them, presently such characters are precisely freaks living *inside* the narrative of "rising" India in terms of self/Other dichotomy, but fundamentally *outside* the social reality, in a different, heterotopian space. There is no longer any desire left to represent them or to construct narratives in which they would deconstruct dominant narratives or to call for social change or emancipation. The freaks are loved, admired and detested simply for what they are—fetishized objects of fascination the spectator has nothing to do with "in real life". They become part of the narrative as long as they stay commodified, as poverty is commodified for the pleasures of exotica consumption.

One may say that on the contrary, such films and the fact that they are made and watched as part of the mainstream signifies an emancipated, more educated public, tired of escapist masala and concerned with the reality of everyday life. It is true, but only to an extent. Who are the intended receivers of these films? Not those who are portrayed in the films or in whose name the heroes fight their battles. These are the same people who make the films, that is, they belong to the same class—urban, educated, emancipated, nouveau riche, upper middle class. But the film-maker is no longer the one who produces a work of art in order to unmask reality. The very fact that such esthetically subversive films become part of the mainstream signifies the transformation of intent. Subversive potential, negativity or what appears to be subversive/negative come back without the antagonistic force, without the "reality", as Marcuse (2002) states.

Preoccupation with the Other in recent Hindi films says quite a lot about the unconscious of *becoming* of global India's self. Indeed, this can be called "Bollywood bourgeois" imaginary, as Dwyer (2006) calls it. It is also possible to call this Other as *the Other* of hyper-industrial state of being, paraphrasing Frow (1997: 72), who, referring to the object of anthropology as the Other of modernity, states that this Other "corresponds to particular tourist objects and experiences—is defined by the absence of design—of calculation or of interested self-awareness. It must therefore exist outside the circuit of commodity relations and exchange values (although it is only accessible through this circuit: one form of the basic contradiction of the tourist experience)."

Thus, we may locate the Other India as a visual tourist object— exotic, alluring, violent and repulsive. Such ambiguous emotions were common features in experiencing the Other in colonial times. Interestingly, such cultural relationships can be observed in a space of postcolonial South among different social classes. As Srivastava (2014: 228) claims, "Indian culture might itself be best imagined as a 'tourist culture' and Indians as permanent tourists within it." He states this with reference to shopping mall design as a negotiation between the global and the local in terms of injecting Indianness as a marketing strategy—ancient India, tribal India, rural India for the consumption of the upper middle class. The importance of the basic fact that the films often portray actual social and political problems should not be taken at face value. Portraying such problems, exposing and interrogating violence, representing the marginal, the subaltern—these are not among the aims of these films. Presenting it as the object of enjoyment is. Enjoying it as a commodity, performing a virtual flânerie or virtual tourist experience is what such films offer.

Walter Benjamin in his discussion on Charles Baudelaire coined the notion of an urban flâneur as a modern individual. In his words, "it is the gaze of the flâneur, whose way of life still conceals behind a mitigating nimbus the coming desolation of the big-city dweller" (Benjamin 2006: 40). The Parisian arcades for him were instrumental in producing the flâneur; without the modern space in the narrow and dirty pavement-less streets, flânerie would have been impossible to conceive. This was the emergence of newness in fin de siècle Paris. "The last journey of the flâneur: death. Its destination: the new", Benjamin (2006: 41) exclaims. Modern space continued to produce different forms of the self throughout the 20th century. Openness, cleanliness and functionality were the destinations of architecture, and here I use architecture not in the strict disciplinary sense. Architecture and architectural space for me is as material as it is mental and imaginary. Ernst Bloch (1988: 186) states, grimly:

> The initial principle of the new architecture was openness: it broke the dark cave. It opened vistas through light glass walls, but this will for balance with the outside world came doubtlessly too early. The de-internalization *(Entinnerlichung)* turned into shallowness; the southern delight for the world outside, while looking at the capitalist external world today, did not turn into happiness. For there is nothing good that happens on the streets, under the sun.

Meanness of the street, mentally dark space, evokes a different kind of spatiality, one that can be called claustrophobic on the one hand and agoraphobic on the other. Spatial fear, as Vidler (1994) demonstrates in his work, became associated with the uncanny. Uncanny emerges as "distancing from reality forced by reality" (Vidler 1994: 6). Friedberg (1994) uses the term "mobilized virtual gaze" in her work. As she argues, it is a "gaze that travels in an imaginary flânerie through an imaginary elsewhere and an imaginary elsewhen" (Friedberg 1994: 2). More than that, such allure signifies transformations in the usage of the imaginary spaces in contemporary "multiplex India". Such branding of India extends into other creative medias producing the carnivalesque— both in actual spaces as well as in imagined ones. This notion refers to the importance of the carnival in the process of becoming modern (also a kind of mediated process of singularization) and can be traced to the pre-modern period and the importance of carnivals, fairs that used to present the participant's dream-like fantasies in the form of the image— the image of *difference*, of the grotesque, the vulgar. Featherstone has analyzed the function the freaks, the lower-class Others and the notion of carnivalesque played in consolidating/singularizing the identity of an emergent class very well (Featherstone 2007), as well as Foucault in his analysis of madness and gazing at the mad as an upper-class pas-time in mental institutions of Paris and London in the 19th century (Foucault 2006). In his dromological analysis, Virilio (2009: 70) states something important for this argument: "speed treats vision like its basic element; with acceleration, to travel is like filming, not so much producing images as new mnemonic traces, unlikely, supernatural". The carnivalesque as a singularizing event, in the environment we may call becoming-postmodern, gives way to acceleration of the gaze, where images flash past, where images of the Other are phenomena the perception of which, on the imaginary, unconscious level, acts as an identity-consolidating matter. The carnival becomes part of visual and mediated perception: it is part of what Virilio (2012: 43) calls the "reality effect". The unconscious is capable of registering such mnemonic traces, even if our movement accelerates. The appearance and instant disappearance of the Other as a reality effect does not negate the fact that the image of the other was reflected and registered.

The very juxtaposition of the newly emergent middle class against its Other and the desire of such imagery contributed to the formation of the middle-class identity, to the process of civilizing. This can, of course, be related to the need of the Other in order to consolidate the self, a notion so important also in postcolonial critique, where civilization consolidated, forged and began to comprehend itself by posing itself against its Other—the Oriental, the savage, the barbarian. This relates to the function of the oriental Other for consolidating the 'Western' self, analyzed by Edward Said (1978), among others. Other India becomes the oriental Other for emergent global India, and the relationship between the two, in the realm of the imaginary, is paradoxically *colonial*.

In short, there was the desire for the Other in order for the civilizing process to begin. What is important for the purpose of my argument is that the carnivalesque of fairs and carnivals, where the affluent ones could experience otherness directly, became transplanted into cinematic image. Therefore, the subaltern carnivalesque in recent Indian films like *Ishqiya* (Abhishek Chaubey, 2010), *Matru ki Bijlee ka Mandola* or *Gangs of Wasseypur* (Anurag Kashyap, 2012) has precisely this function: it acts as a sort of civilizing process for the global, neoliberal India that needs its Other to consolidate its new and not yet fully formed self.

The consumption, usage and function of the new Hindi cinema brand and branded Otherness, with its carnivalesque elements, allow the subaltern masses or Other India to enter the spaces of the upper middle class as imaginary beings and imaginary spaces. The spaces they dwell in and their lives are constructed on screen as imaginary spaces for India that is rapidly transforming. Or, more accurately, a section of India that is transforming, leaving behind its Other, but needing it nevertheless. The function and need of new imaginary spaces reflect the peculiar pattern of development India's urban upper middle class has entered—a development toward postmodernity, toward consumerist culture and different type of esthetics. The ambiguity of "how one should be, how one should think" demands a "common" through which to singularize. New film form gives precisely that.

Newness in the form of new Hindi cinema that is seemingly concerned with social and political issues functions as an integral part of neoliberal consumption. The upper-class elites and their appreciation of this cinema signals its departure from the subaltern mofussil India, which functions as an imaginary space, violent, desired and consolidates urban, neoliberal India's self. At the same time, given the proliferation of actual different spaces (gated communities, shopping malls, multiplexes, sanitized spaces with removed otherness), this new India should not be seen as a rising middle class and emergent civil society in the Euro-American sense. This particular civil society dwells in itself, for itself, and desires to dwell in a globalized space.

Thus, the transformed Hindi cinema consumed by certain groups and classes produces a new type of subjectivity, a new brand of singularity so the subjects would know exactly what to think, and *how to be*.

If we take recent Hindi films as branded products offered by the market, by using them, we become selves, and simultaneously we are offered the image of what kind of Other we should desire on this path. Such is the function of peripheries, small towns and violent spaces. This film form exploits the uncertainties related to class transformations and urban transformations in post-1990s India. The desire for the Other, the reality effect of subaltern carnivalesque and the craving for small-town India are integral parts of complex transformations toward new social imaginary. A social imaginary construction of this involves production of brands; of using these brands to become new selves; of using them in an intensely mediated environment, which is polluted by images of difference and needs the critical gaze of a social ecologist. At the same time, the environment in which the story of global, new India unfolds is polluted, infested with lack—lack that must be satisfied by desiring, by desiring the Other India.

There is no shortage of manifestations of desire for the Other or desire for small town in new Hindi cinema. The vast majority of films play with this notion. Good examples of such imaginary may be the already mentioned *Shanghai* as well as *Matru ki Bijlee ka Mandola*. Bhardwaj's *Haider* (2014) is set in Kashmir, another periphery, a space violent and exotic. But again, Kashmir is only a setting—we have a Shakespearian drama of revenge and violence in a distant space. On the other hand, many film-makers try to negotiate transformations in mofussil India without fetishizing it and often adopting the comedy: *Peepli (Live)* (Anusha Rizvi and Mahmood Farooqui, 2010), *Daayen ya Baayen* (Bela Negi, 2010), Shyam Benegal's works like *Welcome to Sajjanpur* (2008) and *Well Done Abba!* (2009), and Subhash Kapoor's films like *Phas Gaye Re Obama* (2010) and *Guddu Rangeela* (2015), among others.

Interrogating the current fixation on mofussil/rural India, one must ask a broader question: Why do we desire the Other, in a psychoanalytical sense? As Athique and Hill (2010) in their study on the multiplex in India state, the upper class no longer needs a slum-dweller in terms of labor force. This need for a periphery or a slum-dweller or, if we may use a general term, "subaltern" never vanished and has transformed into a different kind of need and moved into the unconscious of becoming postmodern or becoming global of this class. The desire for slum-dweller, subaltern or periphery, both in a geographical sense and philosophical–psychoanalytical sense, has moved into the unconscious of a social class that has not yet emerged fully, that is constantly becoming. The global Indian self is yet to be born, and in order to be born, it must singularize itself in the face of the Other. Here is the need for the Other imaginary, and here is the major difference between the classic New Wave, leftist, politically committed cinema of the 1970s and 1980s and newness emerging in the early 21st century. Srivastava (2014: 115) suggests that the neoliberal state in

India managed to recast "the historical—'developmentalist'—relationship between (middle class) citizens and itself into a consumer-friendly one". Such process, given the nature of neoliberal logic, runs through all practices, including cinematic representations. Mainstream cinema as a product must be consumer-friendly, but the content, the representation, more often than not tends to function within the bounds of being consumer-friendly, rarely crossing the line. And it does not really matter what topic is addressed. Srivastava (2014), in his work, emphasizes the importance of the shopping mall in forming the identity of citizen–consumer. What he leaves out in his analysis is a very important space within the shopping mall, which plays an integral and very important role in subject formation as well—a multiplex.

Lash and Lury (2007) in their work on global culture industries state that in our present age, when media is everywhere, and at the same time, when everything is media, media becomes thingified. It is not only and no longer only about representation and consumption, but navigation; it is not only what media tries to represent to consumers or users, but what users do with media, how do they navigate media and how media gives a helping hand in navigating this complex and transforming brave new world. In the environment of mass media, cultural objects no longer have (or no longer *exclusively* have) cultural value, but use value (Lash and Lury 2007). We are no longer dealing with meaning in terms of representation, but with operationality: what media does and what we do with it. Talking of film, however, it is impossible to leave representation behind. Therefore, we can integrate the two views: film, and the whole genre does represent something, is a commodity, functions as identity-forming media, and at the same time, new Hindi cinema is thingified media and a brand. It produces film-as-navigation, film-as-brand and film-as-thing. This is one of my departure points in understanding the new film form. Lash and Lury look at the problem from the sociological point of view, and I will give their understanding of thing and brand a philosophical twist. In a postmodern or hyperindustrial condition, media gets thingified in the same way works of art have transitioned from modernity to postmodernity for Jameson, producing a "waning of affect in contemporary culture", postmodernity's fixation on surfaces and form without content (Jameson 1991: 17). I think that content is always there, only that the speed at which it transforms and the vertigo effect of the transformational speed produces an inability to grasp, to fully comprehend the content. But if the content is overexposed, blurred due to our bodily and mental motion, it does not mean it is not there. So film becomes a mediated thing under the effect of the postmodern move, and in the postcolonial context of India, this is the result of neoliberal transformations, which made possible the emergence of new urban upper-middle classes, new social imaginaries and new types of mediated experiences.

The films in question, in addition to becoming a brand, manufacture another brand using representation—Other India, small-town India and more generally, otherness. Ravi Vasudevan (2010: 334–61) noted that in the 1990s, Indian popular cinema saw the rise of "nation as brand", something to be consumed outside India. Picking upon the notion of branding of a nation, I would rework it into a different notion—the branding of unruly periphery or violently romantic mofussil India or "slum" India as an imaginary place for consumption by specific social classes in India. Once again: it is not a desire to expose India's social and political problems, not a desire and urgency to interrogate them. It is more a peculiar desire *for* problems represented—problems that are far away from the space occupied by the upper class, and gazing at them creates an enjoyment or 'jouissance' to use a psychoanalytic term.

Branding in this case may refer to the consumption of difference, of otherness, and is an integral part of producing the emergent urban upper class's self. Brands in general tend to produce a "common", a different kind of humanity or a kind of imagined community (Arvidsson 2005: 34). Urban upper class is such an imagined community in the making, and cinema is instrumental in its production. So, desire for the Other and enjoyment in gazing at the Other has an important function in constructing the self of the one who gazes. The proliferation of such functional imaginary spaces in Hindi cinema may be called dromospheric pollution, following Virilio (2008). The imaginary space of cinema can be viewed as such a polluted mediated space, produced by speed and transforming the notion of a journey by giving it multiple

meanings. The workings of such pollution are different in the postcolonial South, and often confined to the imagining and the production
of the upper class' self. Heterotopian space, which is created for this
purpose and which at the same time is the effect of the previously
mentioned processes, is an intermediary space serving the function of
initiating the emergent *global citizens* into globality through consumption. Bernard Stiegler talks of the problems of dis-individuation, and
individuals losing their singularity in a time often labeled postmodern.
He argues that "deprived of their singularity, they attempt to singularize themselves through products suggested by the market" (Stiegler
2014: 60). Thus, becoming self is possible only with the intervention
of the market, which suggests what kind of self should be formed by
offering various products. In this way, the self is constructed, and the
consumption of the same products produces a "community". One could
very productively speak here of urban India's gated communities; one
could also speak of shopping malls and multiplexes aiming at attracting
and thereby producing a *decent crowd* as opposed to subaltern masses
that are filtered so as not to mix with the upper class (Athique and
Hill 2010: 138). But one can also talk of virtual gated community and
de-singularization staged by the cinematic gap. New Hindi cinema's
fixation with the space outside urban India or with India outside the
upper-class milieu produces this gap. But in applying such theories
to India, one should be careful not to generalize: such media-staged
process and consolidation of newness occurs among a reasonably small
group. Guattari (2000) distinguishes three types of ecologies as ethico-
political positions: environmental, mental and social. The most relevant
ones within the confines of this chapter are the last two—mental and
social. He states that integrated world capitalism moves away from
producing goods and services toward "structures producing signs, syn-
tax and—in particular, through the control which it exercises over the
media, advertising, opinion polls, etc.—subjectivity" (Guattari 2000:
47). Guattari is concerned by deterioration and deterritorialization of
social relations under capitalism. This, among other things, produces
Jameson's waning of affect. Guattari calls for a social ecology to counter the effects of mass-media consumption, urban transformations that

in their own right transform and deterritorialize local communities. According to Guattari, mass media de-singularizes individuals, and being singular demands an ecological move (Guattari 2000).

The role and effect of mass media in producing a deterritorialized milieu, a new social class, new social relations and new social imaginary is something we must look at in order to understand the logic of new Hindi cinema. If we look at newness and difference of new Hindi cinema as emancipatory, as producing imaginary concerned with social and political issues in India, we may make a mistake in perceiving these films as kind of *ecological* in their own right. I think that many commentators in the media who write of these films as well as many film scholars fall into this trap. I argue that difference has another function and is anything but an ecological move. The new imaginary provides singularization through the brand of new Hindi cinema.

New Hindi cinema is an imaginary journey, into a space as different as it can get from the lived space of urban upper class, offered by cinema. It is a virtual journey into the wild. It is a kind of navigation in a mediatized world, but cinema and movement with cinema does produce signposts for identity formation. In post-liberalization India's case, urban upper-class identity formation and singularization. So, we must employ quite a few and quite different theoretical positions in order to explain the emergence of new Hindi cinema, its appeal, the timing of its emergence and what this genre says about the transformations of popular culture in the urban upper-class milieu.

A Neurotic Realism?

But we must go deeper into a psychoanalytic reading of new Hindi cinema to understand the relevance of otherness. Slavoj Žižek (2007: 9) says: "It is easy to love one's neighbor as long as he stays far enough from us.... When he comes too near us ... we start to feel his suffocating proximity—at this moment when the neighbor exposes himself to us too much, love can suddenly turn into hatred." This rather simple formula outlining the relationship between the subject and the Other, addressed in a similar fashion by many different scholars, from Lacan to

Derrida, to Bauman and Bhabha, can be understood in several ways. The Other can be seen as the cultural Other or a "subaltern" Other, while the subject is the hegemonic subject wielding the power to represent, power to speak for. Such approach toward otherness, the production of the Other or othering dominates postcolonial theory (Spivak 2010). A subject in this case (which is also produced) is a new Indian middle class, on one hand having the economic power and influence, and on the other, acting as an object of desire for its Others in terms of aspiration to become part of this emergent class.

Understanding the preoccupation of the new Hindi cinema with in-between spaces signals not a desire, but an obstacle in obtaining the object of desire. These obstacles are the spaces existing between the urban middle class's actual location (gated communities, shopping malls, multiplexes, chauffeur-driven cars, etc.) and its mental map; spaces that are uncanny in the sense that they are familiar yet frightening, evoking paranoiac phantasies; spaces of slum-dwellers and pavement-sleepers, of serene village *pastness* phantasms and rural savagery. It demands understanding the shadow of the big Other and its ambivalence, and its importance in constructing a peculiar space of a new self—spaces both actual and mental. Says Slavoj Žižek (2007: 45): "the distance between what we wanted to achieve and the effective result of our activity, the surplus of the result over the subject's intention, is again embodied in another agent, in a kind of meta subject". The meta subject is the big Other, and its ambivalence lies in the fact that the Other is both frightening and reassuring; its existence consolidates the subject. Lacan (1998: 205) states that "the subject depends on the signifier and ... the signifier is first of all in the field of the Other". The nature of the Other is highly ambivalent and contradictory: the Other can be the symbolic order, ideology, God or a perceived enemy in the form of an ethnic or religious minority. A list can go on ad infinitum. Reworking these concepts into "applied" psychoanalysis for cultural critique and understanding the big Other as a cultural Other dwelling in in-between uncanny spaces would help to understand the subject formation of the "world class" in urban India, and its constant distinction vis-à-vis what is outside the imaginary and the actuality of this class. What is outside in this case is in the field of the Other. In our case, the Other can be the imaginary past or "golden age", an ideological concept so often utilized by nationalism as a space-time of origin (romantic villages and North Indian small towns). Or it can be an imaginary present, which is frightening. A present existing in darkness, outside the home space. But the Other can also be understood as ideology, and in our case, neoliberal ideology, a desire to climb up the social and economic ladder, a desire to succeed, a desire to be a global citizen, whatever the meaning of this term might be. A projection of such an ambivalent relationship with the Other is a mental map cinema offers. The narratives of *NH10* and *Highway* oscillate between fear and desire. *NH10* is more interesting psychoanalytically, as an invocation of the Lacanian Other, and *Highway* cleanses the uncanny space by forging a narrative of dependency, a peculiar Stockholm syndrome type of attachment a kidnapped girl Veera develops to her kidnapper, and is more interesting ideologically, as a kind of invocation of the ideological Other.

New Hindi cinema imaginary represents the construction of a neurotic, neoliberal (neuroliberal), urban upper-class subject. This is another point I would like to make in this essay. Engin F. Isin (2004: 223) calls this new self a neurotic citizen, "who governs itself through responses to anxieties and uncertainties", and further claims that "what the neurotic subject wants is the impossible. It wants absolute security. It wants absolute safety. It wants the perfect body. It wants tranquility. It wants serenity. It wants the impossible" (Isin 2004: 232). In his analysis of the neurotic citizen, he argues that neoliberalism transforms bionic citizens into neurotic citizens and, in doing so, transforms itself into neuroliberalism. The neurotic citizen desires what Isin (2004: 232) calls the "impossible", that is, s/he desires an object that is not there, an object created by desire—an object-cause of desire. And it is desiring itself that the subject desires, not the fulfillment of desire. The imaginary object of desire is what Lacan (2017: 168) calls *objet petit a*. The desire circles around the objet petit a without ever attaining it, as this would annul the desire itself—an ultimate tragedy of desiring. Therefore, it is accurate to assume that it is the desire itself that is desired, not the real object, as the object is not real. Absolute safety (or in this case we may even call neoliberal capitalism the big Other of this class) is an impossible goal, and a movement toward the realization of it, a drive. Anxiety in this case may arise when we get too close to the object of desire, or when the circular movement around the objet petit a prevents our desire from being realized.

For my argument, the two dimensions, Isin (2004: 230–1) outlines in which neurosis is played out are important: the home and the border. Both dimensions are related to the duality of self and Other—it is against the Other the home must be protected. It is against the Other the border has to be patrolled. These problems—of the self, of the Other, of home and border—are articulated throughout the new Hindi cinema, the new entertainment or what I would be inclined to call a *neurotic realism*—reality viewed from the perspective of a pathological subject, in the words of M. Madhava Prasad (2007: 89–96).

The home is an ambiguous space for a neurotic subject. Isin (2004: 230) claims that on the one hand, the concept of home as a safe space and homeliness needs to be created in order to constitute such safety and serenity, but on the other, the maintenance of home as a safe bastion under constant threat from the outside space and its horrors produces anxiety and stress. Therefore, home and its protection also become a source of anxiety. In neoliberal/neuroliberal India, such homely spaces are embodied by gated communities, as well as various 'sanitized' non-places of consumption like shopping malls and multiplexes that exclude otherness in the form of lower classes (Bauman 2000; Fernandes 2006; Augé 2008; Athique and Hill 2010; Brosius 2013). While the outside space is the source of fear, home under such a neurotic regime transforms into unhomely or uncanny space. Mazumdar (2002: 71) in her analysis of the uncanny space in Bombay cinema also draws upon "yearning for home and a fear of homelessness", but psychoanalytically, the problem is more complex. As I will discuss later, *NH10* is quite possibly the best cinematic example available of this problem in Hindi cinema. Films like the latter are far from the postmodern celebrations of homelessness and nomadism as body without organs (Deleuze and Guattari 2004). Lewis and Cho (2006: 86), commenting on Deleuze and Guattari and taking Clint Eastwood's "lone gunman" as an example, say that the state of homelessness in this scenario means "lacking a home, but more importantly lacking the desire for a home". Eastwood wanders around a barren landscape, but nomadic wandering is his natural state; he does not desire a home. Lack of desire is crucial in this case, as it is the desire, not the lack of it that is present in *NH10* and similar films. Lack, or the prospect of losing home, being separated from home, having the home invaded by the Other—these are the sources of anxiety reproduced by the neoliberal post-biopolitical regime. Isin (2004: 225) claims that the bionic citizen as a self-sufficient subject that dominated the 20th century and "was governed in and through its freedom" is in tension with another type of citizen who is governed through neurosis. A neurotic citizen desiring safety and serenity might be homeless, but homelessness in this case comes from fear, and is more similar to often-quoted Adornoesque melancholic homelessness—being homeless in one's home (Adorno 2005). Therefore, for a neurotic subject, home is a source of anxiety, while a formless periphery is a source of psychosis, where "the conflict forces the ego to create a new external world that becomes internalized, a delusion" (Isin 2004: 224).

Home as a source of anxiety, albeit in a different sense, is evoked in *Highway* as well. But the frightening outside space, the rural/lower-class periphery in this film, is transformed into precisely the source of serenity. The duality of safety/un-safety, homely/uncanny produces a (post)modern subjectivity based on neurosis, and despite the demand for absolute safety and serenity, no space is fully safe from the gaze of the big Other. The drama of this haunting, a desire without fulfillment, is a source of neurosis, and an unsuccessful movement toward it must be understood as a *drive*. The unattainable object, the object of desire, the cause of anxiety in our case, is *the impossible* absolute safety, which creates what Lacan calls jouissance, enjoyment, a pleasure in pain (Žižek 2007: 56–7). Objet petit a, something appearing to be real, is a support to reality, a "curvature in space itself *which causes us to make a bend precisely when we want to get directly at the object*" (Žižek 2007: 56). Žižek (2007: 56), further explaining Lacan's term and its function related to reality, states that "access to what we call 'reality' is open to the subject *via* the rift in the closed circuit of the 'pleasure principle,' *via* the embarrasing intruder in the midst". Object petit a impedes from within the smooth running of the psyche, but always appears as an external reality. Lacan calls this reality the Real. In the cultivation of the neurotic subject, the existence of uncanny space is an impediment to reach the (unreachable) object of desire—safety and serenity. Anxiety therefore appears as external reality; this so-called "reality" is constructed by the subject in the form of violent space, and fearful others, strangers inhabiting that space. Other space is forged as a heterotopian emplacement, infused with meanings by the subject (other space is everything home space is not), but in the end, it is not external reality. It only has an appearance of one. It is a curious space in-between, a hybrid heterotopia. Foucault (2000) calls heterotopia a semi-real space. In our case, the (unreal) external reality are the fearful features the space is infused with, and the (unreal) features make the desire unattainable. The ultimate tragedy and the source of necessary jouissance is the very fact of desire's unattainability. The Other, in short, has a very clear function in constituting the subject—the neurotic upper-class subject of "shining" India striving for impossible perfection of existence. The Other in this case is an obstacle to enjoyment, as well as it provides meaning and reassurance (it becomes clear what are the sources of fear and suffering). For a neurotic subject, such duality is an absolute necessity. The films in question provide a justification as well as shed light on how things are in neuroliberal India.

NH10

The film is a story of a Gurgaon-based couple Meera (Anushka Sharma) and Arjun (Neil Bhoopalam), and their holiday gone terribly wrong when they leave their safe new middle-class space (which is under a constant threat from the in-between space, of course), and come face to face with the Other in "next-door" rural Haryana, to a destructive end.

The film starts with a car driving through Gurgaon late at night, and an off-screen dialogue between the protagonists. The first five minutes introduce the viewer to a space marking the identity of "shining" India and the new middle class: a bustling metropolis at night, billboards, tall illuminated office buildings and the abundance of markers of globality—shopping malls, a Pepsi stand, a petrol pump with Café Coffee Day in the background, cranes and construction sites, huts with high-rise apartment buildings in the background where the new middle class dwells. The camera here is moving fast and the viewers get the sense of a bustling metropolis on the move. The dialogue happens off-screen and the camera shows who is talking only five minutes into the film. And there is jazz. The speed, the lights and the jazz of a metropolis—this indeed can be any "global city" as there are only few markers of an Indian city during the first scene.

It is the first-half of the film that is most interesting. Initially, the film firmly establishes what Fernandes (2006: 34) calls the "symbolic frames of identity": shopping malls, high-rises, dinner parties, handsomely decorated apartments, cushy corporate jobs. But beneath the surface, throughout the first half-hour of the film, there is inexplicable fear and danger. It first manifests itself after Meera leaves the dinner party alone, late at night, as she has some urgent work to do. She is driving through Gurgaon in her SUV, listening to the radio and stops at the red light. A motorcycle with two men stops next to the car, and the men quietly gaze at her for a moment and then drive off. Few minutes later, the motorcycle blocks the road from the front, and a jeep with more attackers, from behind. The men break the side window of the car, but Meera manages to escape. This is her first encounter with the Other. Later, a police officer explains to Meera and Arjun that the city they live in is like a growing child, and a child does misbehave sometimes.

The film neatly reflects what Isin called the construction of a neurotic citizen and a forging of a culture of fear. He states, drawing upon the often-apocalyptic Mike Davis, that "the risk society undergirded by a culture of fear becomes vulnerable to the emergence of panics, gated communities, security industries and an overall trend toward isolation and insularity" (Isin 2004: 219). Such construction of neoliberal India's neurotic subject is evoked in *NH10*. But the film is ambiguous in evoking clear-cut boundaries separating homeliness and safe space (a high-rise in Gurgaon, an inside space of an SUV) from the uncanny periphery. The boundaries are blurred; they are unstable, constantly shifting. Safe homely space can transform into an uncanny space instantly. The desire for serenity and safety is always there, but this object is never real, unattainable. Whenever neuroliberal subjects think they got closer to that, in the gated communities, inside the secure space of an SUV, the uncanny manifests itself in one way or the other.

In a scene where Meera is attacked by the motorcycle-riding men, fear and anxiety are expressed very well. She hides in the safe space of her SUV, and one of the men smashes her side window. The very fact of motorbike attackers implies that *they* do not need protection from the outside space, as the dark, uncanny space is *their* domain. Meera, on the other hand, feels comfort in the insularity of her SUV.

NH10 creates an atmosphere of safe inside space and menacing outside space very well. It is the safety of an apartment building in Gurgaon as opposed to the street, where men on a motorbike attack Meera. There is also the safety of an SUV inside-space as opposed to the uncanny environment of rural Haryana. But more generally, there is the safety of a city, a space of familiarity and comfort [not to mention that Arjun personally knows the deputy inspector general (DIG) of Delhi police], and the unknowable periphery outside Gurgaon. But more than a blunt statement of home space safety and serenity, Meera and Arjun want to believe in it. Safety is an object of desire with a constant interruption by the Other, which makes the enjoyment of "world-class" living impossible. Therefore, the real uncanny and dark space in this film is the home space, which, can be understood as the Real, externalized by the subject—by Meera and Arjun as their class's representatives.

The first-half of the film is very subtle in evoking the unconscious tensions and the neurotic construction of the new middle class as opposed to the second-half, which unleashes violence and mutual destruction of the subject and the Other.

When Meera and Arjun are leaving the city, they pass a highway tollbooth. This is the boundary separating the metropolis from the periphery. Once they pass this boundary, we can see dark skies and we can hear thunder somewhere in the background. There is also a billboard saying "Have a safe journey", having a measure of irony and acting as a warning and a small preview of what's about to unfold. The film creates a powerful and menacing heterotopian space and populates it with the violent and incomprehensible Other, who, in the film, prove that violent periphery and cunning Other is no mere stereotype.

Let's take as an example a scene I described in detail at the beginning of this chapter. The mirror Meera is looking at, like all rear-view mirrors of the motor vehicles in India, states: Objects in the Mirror are Closer Than They Appear. Psychoanalytically, this scene is perfect to the point of becoming a blunt statement (the director must have read Lacan). The scene is very brief, and despite the drama, which unfolds later in the film, the reflection of the Other leaves an imprint on the unconscious. Meera looks at the Other's reflection with fear and disgust. There is a small "pre-history" to this scene. When Meera and Arjun get lost while trying to find the road to their destination, Arjun stops the car at a roadside dhaba to ask for directions. As he walks over to the men sitting there, Meera stays alone in the car. She sits in the passenger's seat. All of a sudden, a man, a local villager appears next to the side window, and asks if Meera and Arjun were looking for the road to Basantpura, which they were. Meera does not say anything and rolls up the side window. We can see and, to a large extent, understand her fear—she was recently attacked, her illusion of serene life was shattered. The mirror scene happens immediately after, when Arjun comes back to the car. They drive off slowly, and Meera looks at the rear-view mirror and sees a man looking at her. According to Lacan (1998: 257), the mirror stage is crucial for the development of ego, and is a key notion in the Lacanian theory of subjectivity. The mirror stage involves a peculiar "looking-at-the-self" and recognizing the self in the mirror, and is strongly related to narcissism. Lacan calls the "reflection" in the mirror the small other, which is not really other, that is to say, not the radical big Other. For this reason, the scene is interesting in its ambivalence. Taking a cue from postcolonial theory in reworking the Other as symbolic order into cultural Other, we may conclude as Bhabha (2004: 122) does in saying that "colonial mimicry is the desire for a reformed, recognizable Other, *as a subject of a difference that is almost the same, but not quite*". Herein lies the ambivalence of the object in the mirror, which is "closer than it appears"; on the one hand, Meera sees a specular image, that is, a projection of her ego or the little other, but on the other hand, she sees the Other, which "is almost the same, but not quite". The latter problem, according to Bhabha (2004: 127), is "a form of difference that is mimicry". If we replace Bhabha's "colonial" with neuroliberal, we can conclude that mimicry is the desire for a reformed, recognizable Other, and in our case, in the form of the peripheral object belonging to an altogether different India, Other India, which is part of the object of desire, that is, safety and serenity. Otherness in this case is desired on several levels: it is desire for a reformed Other, and a reform, the undoing of otherness, would mean the elimination of threat, and this would correspond to the object of desire. At the same time, the Other is desired per se, because it justifies the drive toward the object of desire. Žižek (2007: 45), in his analysis of this problem qua Nazism and the figure of a Jew, states that the Other's radical ambivalence "can function as a quieting and strengthening reassurance ... or as a terrifying paranoiac agency". As I mentioned before, the "embarrassing intruder" prevents one from enjoying, but creates jouissance, a pleasure in pain.

Therefore, Meera is enjoying the impossibility of attaining the object of desire; she desires the desire itself. Something similar, but far less radical, happens in *Highway*, as we shall see, but otherness in that film is of a more ideological nature than in *NH10*.

There is one more very important scene in the film, when Meera tries to get help from the local police. Not only is she termed as "English-type madam" by a rural police officer—as she belongs to what can be called a "Delhi upper class", therefore she is not simply a city dweller, but English, or more broadly, a foreign type—but another officer explains to her that "your democracy ends with the last shopping mall". This is a very interesting thing to say. It evokes the shopping mall as a marker of neoliberal lifestyle. Even more, a shopping mall stands as a symbol not only of prosperity, being a "world class" or English type, but also it is a code word for democracy. The shopping mall as a symbolic frame of identity is indeed, in this case, projected as a last bastion of civilization at the edge of an unruly and violent periphery. At the same time, the fact that Meera is using quite a lot of English words and is described as an English type emphasizes the English language as shaping the "symbolic frames of identity" of the new Indian middle class. It is part of the knowledge needed in gaining access to the membership to this class (Fernandes 2006: 34). Something similar also happens in *Highway*, but there the contact with otherness has an emancipatory effect.

Highway

Highway is a very good example of urban center/rural periphery spatial configuration, and is one of the best recent examples in Hindi cinema of becoming self and the need of a lower social class to do so. Like *NH10*, *Highway* is also a peculiar road movie offering a movement through space, a movement which has a transformative effect. As opposed to *NH10*'s horror in the face of the Other, in *Highway*, the Other is violent and threatening, but is instrumental for the urban self in order to discover what we could call the *meaning of life*. I would call this film pseudo-Marxist in terms of the love and affection shown by the new middle class toward the lower class. Pseudo, because there is no love, affection and care, only selfish motives informing the desire for the Other.

The plot of this film is rather simple. Veera (Alia Bhatt), a girl in her early 20s, lives in Delhi with her parents. Her father is rich and influential. She is getting ready to marry a young man from her social class. But later on, in the film, we learn that her upper-class home space is far from ideal. Beyond the shiny façade, there is trauma and repressed memories of childhood sexual abuse. And the upper class, the parents and Veera's fiancé, are portrayed as greedy, insensitive, ignorant and demonstrate the lack of understanding of "what life is all about". One night, when driving with her fiancé through Delhi, Veera gets kidnapped for ransom and is taken to a village outside Delhi. To cut the long story short, Veera slowly begins to develop an attachment to her kidnapper, a rough in-between space dweller Mahabir (Randeep Hooda). Slowly, she stops being afraid and herself asks, "What is happening to me?" She begins to appreciate life on the highway, life on the run, a peculiar nomadic wandering. From Rajasthan, Mahabir takes her to Punjab and, after that, to Himachal Pradesh. At the very end of the film, she states that her life in Delhi was prison, which basically means that the encounter with the fearsome Other, a man from the peripheries and also beyond the law, had a liberating effect. We can analyze this film from an ideological perspective. The Other in this film has a clear function: to liberate Veera from the *prison of new middle-class existence*. When he accomplishes his goal, the police track them down and Mahabir is shot to death.

Žižek in his analysis of Hollywood films gives an example of *Titanic* (James Cameron, 1997). Just like *Titanic*, *Highway* focuses on the transgression of the class divisions. Paraphrasing Žižek (2008: 58), Veera is "a spoiled high-society girl in an identity crisis: she is confused, does not know what to do with herself, and, much more than her lover, Di Caprio is a kind of 'vanishing mediator' whose function is to restore her sense of identity and purpose in life, her self-image ... once his job is done, he can disappear". Mahabir, of course, is a very different type of vanishing mediator. As opposed to Jack Dawson (Leonardo Di Caprio), who is an excessively lovable working-class man, Mahabir is a self-described "dog-who-would-die-a-dog's-death". He is similar to the violent and bloodthirsty Haryana savages as depicted in *NH10*, but he gradually transforms into a savage we, just as Veera, are bound to like far more than the selfish, cold high-society Delhiites. In turn, he transforms Veera and injects into her a desire for a different life, even though this is a pure fantasy. At the end of the film, Mahabir vanishes when his job is done—the police shoot him.

Žižek, in his analysis of *Titanic*, claims that such need of a contact with the lower class to refresh the upper class's blood is a necessity in bourgeois imaginary. Lower classes, the proletariats, are perceived as knowing what the joys of life are. They are more alive than the bourgeoisie, closer to the soil. But this is the exploitation of the lower class. Veera exploits Mahabir, and the road trip into the peripheries is a fantasy serving her own purposes: she wants to refresh herself, to inject liveliness into her stale life among the Delhi upper class. When she gets what she wants, the Other must die; the vanishing mediator vanishes. Indeed, if Veera and Mahabir were to live happily ever after in the film, the reality of life in the mountains and "the misery of everyday life would soon have destroyed their love" (Žižek 2008: 58). Of course, there is no love as such in *Highway*; at least, there is no ordinary love story. There is, however, a different type of desire—a desire of/for the Other. Having said that, one scene at the end of the film is very interesting. Veera and Mahabir reach Himachal Pradesh and are allowed to stay at a small house, alone. This is Veera's dream come true—to live in a house in the mountains, in the middle of nowhere, to live in freedom. When they move into the house, Veera pushes Mahabir out, so she could clean the house and cook food. She assumes the role of a partner or a wife. Mahabir secretly watches her doing that and starts crying, because he is reminded of his mother whom he has not seen in a very long time. Veera comes out, sees Mahabir crying and begins to comfort him. In that moment, she assumes the role of Mahabir's mother. After that, they go back to the house and spend the night together. We do not know what happens in the house at night. We do know that they sleep together, but the question if they have a sexual relationship similar to the relationship in *Titanic*, that is left for us to figure out. In the next scene, we are shown the morning in the mountains. Mahabir is killed and Veera is saved.

There are many other films that evoke a sense of a predatory city, like *No One Killed Jessica* (Raj Kumar Gupta, 2011), both in terms of the narrative and Rani Mukerji's voice-over at the beginning of the film, where she states that Delhi is about power. But this is a very different city from the one constructed in *NH10*. *Highway* follows a romantic periphery tone. Yes, the Other is menacing but, in the end, is instrumental in constructing a new self. In this sense, *NH10* (and the title itself refers to a highway—National Highway No. 10) is far stricter in creating a binary of self and Other. It is more evocative in portraying neoliberal India as an uncanny space of a particular social class, one that Meera and Arjun of *NH10* belong to.

What all such different films do is offer an imaginary journey to exotic far-flung spaces. It allows us to cast the mobilized virtual gaze onto the Other (Friedberg 1994). It is the violent virtual gaze of misrepresentation and consumption of the Other. This Other has a very important function to perform. The space in which this fable unfolds is far from realistic; it is possible to call it a heterotopian space, a space both real and unreal, to invoke once again Foucault's (2000) notion. The films constructing such space, the other space, constantly project themselves as being transgressive and dissenting. Despite a possibility to distinguish between more mainstream films by someone like Bhardwaj and more offbeat ones by Banerjee and others, the effect produced by all these films is the same. In a theoretical analysis of this film form and form flow, it may be useful to look at a film as a thing, and the emergent genre as a constantly transforming cluster of brands: something integral to hyper-industrial consumption.

3

HAUNTING AND UNCANNY CITIES
OF NEOLIBERAL INDIA

In this chapter, I will not go into the history of horror cinema in India. There are several good studies on this cinematic phenomenon (Sen 2017; Dhusiya 2018). I shall address only one aspect of it that is crucial to understanding urban and cinematic transformations—the haunted spaces of the city. I shall primarily focus on several works by two film-makers: Ram Gopal Varma, who was central to the rise of dark cinematic imagination in the 1990s, and Pawan Kripalani, a younger generation film-maker, who made his debut in 2011 with *Ragini MMS*. The chapter concludes with a discussion on *Talaash*, a film that merges a theme of haunting with film noir.

Dark City as a Site and Source of Imagination

Urban transformations, such as massive urban expansions, redevelopment projects, the rise of shopping mall culture, luxury apartment buildings, development of the so-called "satellite towns" like Gurugram and Noida in the National Capital Region, presence of international branded commodities and overall development of consumer culture as well as neoliberal economy's march in the rural and small-town India, foreign direct investment (FDI) and land grabbing, deforestation and dispossession making way for economic greatness—all of it, just like most social, political and cultural issues at any given time anywhere in the world, is seldom absent from cinema. What in the official history is seen as a period of euphoria and India's entry onto the world stage as an economic superpower, or "awakening giant", in cinematic language is translated as nightmarish and as the dark reality beneath the smooth surface of neoliberal triumphalism. The interior space of neoliberal restructuring, coupled with increasing social divide, communal and caste tensions, the development of the precariat—in the words of Guy Standing (2011)—and transforming culture with its multiple byproducts is the source for contemporary cinematic imagination, be it critical or affirmative.

The city is the quintessential site of the production of new subjects, new sensibilities and imaginations in post-liberalization India, as many authors point out (Fernandes 2006; Srivastava 2007, 2014; Athique and Hill 2010; Brosius 2014). According to Srivastava (2014: 107), the consolidation of middle-class identity in the city relates to two ideas: "spatial engendering of consumer-citizen and entrepreneurial sensibility" and the idea of "'securing' spaces". The first idea manifests itself as a shopping mall, the second as a gated community, as an enclave. Engin F. Isin (2002: 42–3, emphasis mine) claims that "groups cannot materialize themselves as real without realizing themselves in space, without creating configurations of buildings, patterns, and arrangements, and *symbolic representations of these arrangements*". Precisely the realm of symbolic is crucial for my understanding of emergent Hindi film forms and cinema of anxiety as a symbolic representation of social relations under neoliberalism "Place-image" or the symbolic meaning of space is produced both by interaction with space and spatial relation to other sites (Shields 1991: 60). Ravi Sundaram (2010: 2) suggests that "postcolonial cities today are also media cities". Drawing upon Walter Benjamin's ideas on the urban experience and technology, he emphasizes the blurring of lines separating the urban experience and the media in post-liberalization India.[1] Media to him, including cinema,

---

[1] Dibakar Banerjee's *Love, Sex aur Dhokha* (2010) is the only example in Indian cinema that attempts to blur the lines between media and the urban experience.

transforms the very perception of phenomena in the city. He states that "this changed phenomenology of nearness and distance brought about by the media has a productive and equally dark, visceral quality, tearing apart stable modes of contemplation" (Sundaram 2010: 5).

The media experience and mediatization of life underwent significant shifts. Media consumption and cinema consumption changed in many ways—in terms of the introduction of satellite and cable television (TV) channels, the rise of advertisement industries and availability of foreign goods. This book focuses on the particular forms of cinema consumed by what could be termed as the elite urban population. The Other of the affluent city dweller is in no way marginal in terms of consumption and the desire for the new; only the consumption is marked by illegality, vernacularization and innovation (Abbas 2008; Mukhopadhyay 2012; Paul 2016). Or, what Sundaram (2010: 12) calls "pirate urbanism", claiming that "new liberalism produced pirate urbanism as an illegal postcolonial descent into hell, a reason for globalization's impurity in India".

The emergence of new types of cinematic imagination must be seen in the context of transforming economic, political, social and cultural landscape in post-liberalization India, as was mentioned before. The effect of television both in terms of strengthening the populist attitudes and reflecting the unease of the Hindu middle class has been seen before the advent of cable and satellite TV (Mankekar 1999b; Rajagopal 2008). The 1990s marked India's entry into the space of full-fledged consumption. While it is possible to speak of the multitude of transformation, I would like to emphasize several of them: the increasing presence of diaspora and diasporic space as a source of a particular imagination of "global India"; the entry of a quintessential space of consumption—a shopping mall—which must be viewed as a material source of imagination of globality and affluence; the emergence of multiplex cinema facilitating the distribution of off-mainstream cinema; the proliferation of gated communities and stricter spatial segregation in the cities in terms of wealth and affluence.

Mazumdar (2010: 156) calls the new film form an "Urban Fringe", and states that "like a virus, the Fringe exists alongside the delirium of globalization today, portraying space as a bad object". It is a cinema of globalization; it is starkly different from the "new wave" of the 1970s in terms of the clear-cut political message and "mission" the latter cinema had, but I believe the present new Hindi cinema constructs a new type of realism, delirious realism, or, as I will call it later in the book, neurotic realism. But I think that instead of seeing the new form as a *fringe*, it is more useful to employ another concept—*X-urbanism* (Abbas 2008). Abbas uses this concept in his analysis of transforming Hong Kong and Shanghai, and emphasizes the emergence of a suburban city that ceases being suburban, that is, transforms from fringe into the Other of the city, mirroring it, but being starkly different from it. He explains that:

> Unlike the suburban city, X-urbia develops not in opposition to the center, but in contiguity and in tandem with it. We thus find an urbanism that does not oppose fringe to center, home to workplace, but rather that is multi-centered, decentered, or fractal. X-urbia does not supplement the suburban city, but supplants it, changing it from the inside out. (Abbas 2008: 247)

In India, probably the best example of such X-urbia is Gurugram, the so-called millennium city in the national capital region, south-west of Delhi in the state of Haryana, sometimes referred to as Delhi's satellite town. Several issues are important here. I would see Gurugram both as an actual space and an imaginary space, a heterotopia of the new middle class, therefore, both a mental space and a material one. While the city is a source of imagination and a lifeline of the new film form, employing the understanding of urbanism and urban transformation are very helpful in understanding cinema. It is not because the cinema represents the city. It is not always so anyway. It is because the materiality of the city and the existence of X-urbia as a heterotopian emplacement of the new middle class, or more precisely, middle classness as a feeling, mirrors the ephemeral imaginary of cinema.

The fringe does not oppose itself to the center; it is not a periphery, not an alternative to the existing urbanity. "X" marks the unknown, or perhaps unrepresentable—a quality that is very important in understanding new Hindi cinema. X-urbia, both actual and cinematic, illustrates the collapse of binary between the center and the periphery. Such blurring of strict lines and seemingly relaxed esthetic hierarchy can be understood as undecidable, or *pharmakon* to use Jacques Derrida's (1981: 95–117) term—as a thing, a concept, which can have two different and opposing qualities in itself escaping hierarchy, compartmentalization. At the same time, its constant flow, mutation and undecidability can also signify and does signify the neoliberal logic of pushing the boundaries of what is acceptable (Deleuze and Guattari 2004: 267).

The city as a ubiquitous site is one of the key objects of new Hindi cinematic imagination. Apart from noir imagery, many other films and film-makers treat the Indian metropolis as a site of violent negotiations of neoliberal subjectivities, like *Kaminey* (Vishal Bhardwaj, 2009), *Titli* (Kanu Behl, 2014), *Talvar* (Meghna Gulzar, 2015), *Pink* (Aniruddha Roy Chowdhury, 2016), or critically represent the everyday life in a transformed urban space, like Dibakar Banerjee's *Khosla ka Ghosla* (2006) and *Oye Lucky! Lucky Oye!* (2008), *Life in a Metro* (Anurag Basu, 2007), *Do Dooni Char* (Habib Faisal, 2010), *Vicky Donor* (Shoojit Sircar, 2012), *Hindi Medium* (Saket Chaudhary, 2017), among many others.

Thus, the new esthetic form may be seen as a deterritorialized flow, and undecidable—a phenomenon escaping the firm grasp of a film scholar or cinema anthropologist. This form also functions in a highly advanced media environment, integrating not only films themselves but also the spaces in which the films are consumed and the networks through which they proliferate. This would call for an empirical research in film consumption in urban areas, but that is not the objective of this book. Rather, I would like to make use of Paul Virilio's notion of dromology or the science of speed (Virilio 2008). The speed at which we move through physical space and media space has a blurring effect and we find it more difficult to grasp phenomena around us. Speed transforms our bodily and mental perception of phenomena because our bodily/mental positioning changes too rapidly. Fredric Jameson found it difficult to grasp this dromological transformation and termed the evasive perception as "pastiche", as the "waning of affect in contemporary culture" (Jameson 1991: 17). His "statue with blind eyeballs" does not necessarily have blind eyeballs; the latter are just beyond perception (that is, they are not *visible*) using the intellectual tools we are accustomed to utilize in analyzing changing cultural form.

Uncanny Genealogies

The speed at which spaces and the relations with spaces individuals have transform can produce feelings or affects, first and foremost, signified by fear, paranoia and dread. And also spaces of "fundamental insecurity: that of a newly established class, not quite at home in its own home" (Vidler 1994: 3–4). Transforming urban space, as well as transforming esthetic sensibilities and senses of belonging can produce affect similar to one identified by Vidler in his exploration of modern architectural uncanny. Drawing upon Freud's conceptualization of the uncanny, he claims:

> From the 1870s on, the metropolitan uncanny was increasingly con-flated with metropolitan illness, a pathological condition that potentially afflicted the inhabitants of all great cities; a condition that had, through force of environment, escaped the overprotected domain of the short story. The uncanny here became identified with all the phobias associ-ated with spatial fear, including "la peur des espaces" or agoraphobia, soon to be coupled with its obverse, claustrophobia. (Vidler 1994: 6)

From the "overprotected" space of short stories by E.T.A. Hoffmann and Edgar Allan Poe, the uncanny found its way into the emergent cities of the 19th and early 20th centuries, and very soon found its way back into the imagination, this time in the form of cinema. Ranjani Mazumdar (2002: 71) in writing on the uncanny in Bombay cinema of the late 20th to early 21st century states that "the uncanny emerges within a tense space where the yearning for a home and a fear of home-lessness constantly impinges on desire and freedom. Thus, the homely, the domestic and the nostalgic are constantly placed under threat."

According to Freud, the uncanny is an esthetic category within the boundaries of "all that is terrible". There is, however, a thin line

separating *heimlich* and *unheimlich*, homely and unhomely (uncanny):
"Thus *heimlich* is a word the meaning of which develops toward an
ambivalence, until it finally coincides with its opposite, *unheimlich*.
Unheimlich is in some way or other a sub-species of *heimlich*" (Freud
1985: 339). Uncanny, according to Vidler (1994: 11), is in the "aesthetic dimension" of space, and is a "representation of a mental state
of projection that precisely elides the boundaries of the real and the
unreal in order to provoke a disturbing ambiguity, a slippage between
waking and dreaming". He tracks the uncanny to the transforming cities of the 19th century; to Paris of Baudelaire "losing himself in the
swarming boulevards" to "urban estrangement" as a "consequence of
the centralization of the state and the concentration of political and
cultural power" (Vidler 1994: 4). Then there is Walter Benjamin and
the flânèrie in Parisian arcades, Georg Simmel and Zygmunt Bauman's
"strangers", and ultimately, the amorphous, *liquid* hybrid city in perpetual transformation due to the global flows of capital. But another
esthetic moment is relevant before delving into the cities, both actual
and cinematic: a type of imagination that is deeply unsettling, para-
noid and nihilistic; imagination that speaks of more than the urban
estrangement—film noir. Fear of spaces here, either agoraphobia or
claustrophobia, must be understood as social anxiety, the social space
fear that is produced by transforming urban spaces, be it gentrification, influx of migrant laborers into growing and expanding cities or
the emergence of what Marc Augé (2008) termed non-places. Esther
Cheung (2009: 105), writing on Hong Kong and drawing upon Vidler's
notion of architectural uncanny, introduces the term "ghostly city"
aiming to trace the "ambiguous contemporary sensibility produced by
urban mutations". Ghostliness for her is a reference to the "exploration
of homelessness". Or, in other words, not the actual homelessness, but
unhomeliness. Ghostliness and homelessness at one's own home are
some of the crucial points: the notion of "home" signifies the serene,
secure, homely (*heimlich*) space, while "not-being-at-home"—its
opposite or unhomely (*unheimlich*). Freud (1985: 342), in defining the
uncanny, states that it is "what once was *heimisch*, homelike, familiar;

the prefix 'un' is the token of repression". On the one hand, transformation is inherent in the very notion of uncanny—unhomely emerges in the process of transforming homeliness. On the other hand, because homely has been associated with private space hidden from the public view, it was always equally a space of anxiety. What is concealed is not necessarily an idealized serene space. On the contrary, what is repressed behind the closed doors, outside the conscious knowledge, can be sheer terror and the source of anxiety. Thus, according to Vidler (1994: 167), such "space is assumed to hide, in its darkest recesses and forgotten margins, all the objects of fear and phobia that have returned with such insistency to haunt the imaginations of those who have tried to stake out spaces to protect their health and happiness". For Heidegger (1968), the fundamental meaning of dwelling is preserving, sparing and being at peace. To dwell is to spare; it is to be at peace. He contrasts this with building, which does not necessarily produce dwelling. "We do not dwell because we have built, but we build and have built because we dwell" (Heidegger 1968). Dwelling and building are not juxtaposed—building is only possible because of dwelling. Similarly, homely is possible only because of the uncanny. Building produces an uncanny feeling when it is dislocated from dwelling, when it has the features of a non-place, when it is not yet produced as part of dwelling, if we could see dwelling in Bourdieu's (1977) sense of the habitus. Through spatial performance, the spatial competence is cultivated and building becomes dwelling, losing its uncanniness. But these are ideal categories. Because, as *heimlich* and *unheimlich* are inseparable and occur simultaneously in the same space, dwelling itself can produce the uncanny. If we see dwelling as similar to habitus in terms of its properties, and if habitus is constantly transforming, as Bourdieu claims, which implies velocity, and if we hold, following Virilio, that speed and space form a continuum, and that the late modern age is about acceleration, then we can see dwelling as unstable, shifting and therefore provoking uncanniness. Therefore, dwelling does not guarantee being at peace; on the contrary, it can impose violence on the subject, be it physical violence or mental one, the violence of fear and anxiety.

Haunted City

Cheung (2009: 107) writes on "ghostly chronotopes" and claims that they "articulate a specific structure of feeling defined by a sense of dislocation". Such a chronotope demonstrates a close relationship between the world as represented and the real work of transforming Hong Kong's urban space. Ghostly, she says, while analyzing the social context of Hong Kong horror cinema, is what is "repressed and invisible in the global, celebratory discourse" (Cheung 2009: 105). Such "ghostly chronotopes" and variously haunted spaces are central also in Hindi cinema. Similar processes can be observed elsewhere in Asia, especially in South Korea, where horror cinema has deep traditions. The spaces, both allegorical and material in which the narratives of films unfold, be these horror films or other examples of dark imagination, are the spaces produced, in one way or the other, by transnational capital and neoliberalism. More than that, these transformations tend to be more or less uniform. Given that emergent Hindi film form in general is the cinema of globalization, the transcultural influences on it are unde-niable, and East Asian horror, East Asian noir cinema as transnational commodities, do flow both globally and within Asia (Smith 2013; Lee and Kolluri 2016). Horror or gothic is a far more organic manifestation of the uncanny, and it is closely related both to Freud's conceptualiza-tion and to the psychological experience of fear.

Spectrality as a conceptual metaphor and as an analytical tool is a notion sometimes considered as being more "scholarly" than ghost-liness. Popularized by Jacques Derrida, who also coined the notion of "hauntology" in *Specters of Marx* (2006), in the light of the col-lapse of the Union of Soviet Socialist Republics (USSR) and Francis Fukuyama's end of history thesis, they both offer interesting insights into the uncanny and haunting nature of global capitalism. The subject of hauntology is a being that is not fully present. As Mark Fisher (2012: 19) explains, it is simultaneously *no longer* and *not yet*. It also refers to the erosion of spatiality, and to the rise of non-places and non-times.

To Avery Gordon (2008: xvi), the "specters or ghosts appear when the trouble they represent and symptomize is no longer being con-tained, or repressed, or blocked from view". Ghostliness often manifests itself as a past impossible to contain, and which comes back to haunt the forgetfulness of the present. It is the ghostliness that emerges in the life of Saajan Fernandes in *The Lunchbox*, who, after establishing contact with a woman who is more imaginary than real, who dwells in the lunchbox and in the letters and in dreams, begins to reflect upon his own life and memory: memory of his childhood, of his wife, of the city that he no longer recognizes. Ila is a woman not fully present, but at the same time, her spectral presence triggers the awakening of Saajan to the past still haunting the present. The newness, the ephemerality and *forced* forgetful nature of the present repress history into the spatial unconscious by producing the transience of non-place. Hauntology, Mark Fisher claims, marks the erosion of spatiality and time. Haunting, according to him, occurs "when a place is stained by time, or when a particular place becomes the site for an encounter with broken time" (Fisher 2012: 19). In a more direct sense, the "staining" of a place by time, in the modern imagination since Edgar Alan Poe, often manifests itself as a haunted house.

Raat and *Bhoot*

Ram Gopal Varma, Bollywood's bête noire, who can be considered as one of the dark fathers of new Hindi cinema, conjures up the very literal gothic ghostliness in many of his films—*Raat* (1992), *Bhoot* (2003), *Phoonk* (2008), *Bhoot Returns* (2012), among others. Interestingly, as if confirming the close connection of film noir and horror via the concept of uncanny, his films can be seen as falling into two broad categories— horror films and noir films.

Raat and *Bhoot*, both focusing on haunted houses and the dead haunting the living, are interesting in terms of the timing of their releases and in their material representations. *Raat* was released in 1992, in the immediate aftermath of liberalization, when the transformation of sensibilities, and neoliberalism's relationship with the past and with difference was yet to be consciously materialized. It is set in Hyderabad, an upcoming city, a city that, together with Bangalore, rose into prominence because of neoliberal reforms, injunction of foreign capital and the emergence of "tech hubs" in South India. The film anticipates what we, a decade later, shall see in *Bhoot*: a more solid, more concrete middle-class sensibility and the sense of the uncanny. The uncanny in *Raat* is raw. The ghost haunts, but in a very direct, brutal manner. A middle-class family moves into a new house in the suburbs of Hyderabad. Soon after, strange things begin to occur. As we know, uncanny refers more to strangeness than to outright fear, to things and occurrences that should not be, that are out of place and therefore seem out of joint. Minnie (Revathy), the college-going daughter of an industrialist, starts seeing things, feeling things. Years ago, a man and his lover lived in the house, and suddenly the woman disappeared. As is explained in the climax of the film, she was murdered by the man in the house and her spirit remained. The ghost possesses Minnie, and, before anyone notices this, she kills her best friend, a police officer investigating the killing and attempts to murder her father. Initially, the family tries to deal with this with the help of modern medicine—psychiatry. But simultaneously, the indigenous knowledge, something that does not belong, should not belong to the rational, science-based present, is called upon to make sense of the present's strangeness. A *tantric* is called upon to exorcise the ghost. In the end, the past is exorcised by the past knowledge in terms of not belonging to the rational, globalized present. But the past stains the present with trauma that makes the project of the present imperfect, flawed. The film climax scene is very evocative. Minnie is in her bedroom, bed-ridden, delirious. A psychiatrist attends to her, without any success and injects sedatives into her veins. Simultaneously, another battle with strangeness for Minnie's body and soul is happening, quite literally, in the underground. The tantric and Minnie's boyfriend discover a tunnel where the ghost possessing Minnie dwells. Two battles ensue simultaneously: one on the surface, an attempt to deal with spectrality in rational and modern terms; the other, below the surface, with the help of the knowledge that itself is spectral. The present does not, cannot accept the existence of spectrality. Spectrality and those experiencing it are the subjects of psychiatry.

Neoliberalism in its attempt to forge new subjectivities and new moral universes strives to both negate and purge differences and alternatives, or else to incorporate them using commodification—a process that Marcuse (2002) effectively criticized as the construction of one-dimensional thought. Differences, multiplicities and alternatives can be interpreted as specters—material and mental presences either commodified or pushed underground, but not erased, built-over, re-populated. Darkness arising from the uncanny presence of absence becomes darkness only because it is juxtaposed, imagined as such, in a binary so common for post-enlightenment, Eurocentric thought. In horror films like *Raat*, such darkness manifests itself not only as a ghostly presence of the unthinkable, but also in the attempts to deal with such spectral presence—something that the battle between rational/irrational, psychiatrist/tantric reflect both in *Raat* and *Bhoot*. Indigenous knowledge manifested as a tantric in this sense haunts the globalized, one-dimensional world view. But in the end, the Other of the global—if we read "global" as part of Westernization project—is reconciled with the "global knowledge" by producing a hybrid space, where differences can be accommodated as work with the dominant narrative. In *Raat's* case, understanding Minnie's condition as possession, and not as mental illness. The psychiatrist heals the body by applying sedatives, while the tantric heals the soul by exorcising the ghost. At the end of the film, after the ghost has been exorcised, the psychiatrist, while leaving the house, explains the further steps of mental recovery in English to the father, while the mother sits with the tantric at the dining table and asks him "What is *it?*". The tantric explains thus:

When the darkness of the night falls, we light a lamp. It does not dispel the darkness; rather, a limited sphere of space gets illuminated with the light. However, we often tend to forget that nature has hidden innumerable unknown truths in that endless darkness that surrounds us beyond this sphere of brightness. We should be aware of the presence of that darkness—still inaccessible to human knowledge. Perhaps a day will come when human knowledge will be able to decipher the mystery of this darkness, too.

His explanation illustrates the unstable relation between homely and uncanny very well. Still, *Raat* operates within a matrix of binary oppositions—darkness and light, science and occult, modernity and tradition, and therefore fails to grasp the complexity of the uncanny.

Bhoot, a peculiar remake of *Raat*, offers an extreme and very literal representation of a haunted space. Swati (Urmila Matondkar) and Vishal (Ajay Devgn), an upper-middle-class couple, move into a luxury apartment in Mumbai, located in a high-rise where the ghosts of the past, of murdered dwellers, reside. *Bhoot* is very similar to *Raat* in terms of narrative: a middle-class family moves into a new home, where a woman and her young son were murdered sometime back. Swati starts developing the feeling of a presence that should not be there; her condition deteriorates; a psychiatrist is called upon; and later, when "rational" and contemporary measures are of no use, a tantric. As in *Raat*, the rationality of Western globalization is reconciled with indigenous knowledge, only that the former is far more pronounced in *Bhoot*. The middle-class representatives, especially Vishal, are more conscious of it. As opposed to a bungalow in the suburbs of Hyderabad, the haunted space is a luxury apartment in Mumbai—one of the spaces marking the middle-class sensibilities and strife for safety and serenity in a high-rise building, above and beyond the seething postcolonial metropolis.

One scene, which mirrors itself in both films, is of special importance. In *Raat*, Minnie and her friends go to a cinema and engage in what perhaps could be termed as a rudimentary "global" movie-going experience, involving popcorn and Thums Up. During the film, the cinema hall transforms into a strange and unfamiliar space for Minnie; all the people, including her friends, are gone, as she finds herself sitting alone. She, then, gets transported to some other space, before returning to the cinema hall as if nothing had happened. In *Bhoot*, Vishal suggests to Swati that they go out to watch the Hollywood movie, *Spiderman*. They go to a multiplex, and during the movie, in the dark, Swati notices that all the spectators in the hall are facing her, staring. Their faces are not of living humans. She screams, tries to escape, runs out into the multiplex hall, but is being followed. And then she wakes up in her uncanny apartment, in her bed, next to her husband. The apartment and the ghosts residing there are trying to possess her.

What is interesting about this scene is not only the sense of terror when faced with something that should not be there, should not be happening, but the spatiotemporal distance separating the two films. While in 2003, Swati and Vishal go to a multiplex, in 1992, there still were none, and Minnie and her friends were watching a film at a single-screen theater. The multiplex, apart from being an exclusive space for a particular film-going crowd, is a crucial material space in the development of new Hindi cinema. The emergence of multiplexes with multiple screens made it possible for the "alternative" cinema to be screened. The emergence of the multiplex in India began around 1995, and its development was an integral part of changing consumption patterns and of transforming urban space. Its emergence occurred during the euphoria surrounding India's economic boom, in the immediate post-liberalization period. Gopal (2011) terms the initial rise of the multiplexes as the first-generation ones (1995–2004), and claims that the first-generation multiplex "was concerned with the creation of a film grammar that would make possible the enunciation of a new middle-class cinema" while the second-generation films "are entrusted with broadening the audience of the multiplex film to include the proliferating middle classes in all of urban India". *Bhoot* was released in 2003, therefore, at the end of the first generation. The multiplex, crucially, also had another grammatological function: it was designed to accommodate a particular audience—upper class, richer, so that they would not need to mix with the masses at the single-screen cinemas, which was the case for decades till the late 1990s. The multiplex, thus, acted as a space excluding otherness in terms of social class; it was an emic space, to use Bauman's (2000) phrase. It was a space having a particular ambience and safety, and offered a possibility to mix only with the people of a certain social standing. The Other of the upper middle class, therefore, was conveniently left outside by a relatively high ticket price (Athique and Hill 2010). New Hindi cinema establishes contemporary India's dark side as an esthetically constructed mise-en-scene, and *Bhoot* illustrates this claim very well. The Other, in this case a ghost, interrupts the pleasures of upper-class living and transforms what was supposed to be a safe space into an extreme and life-threatening uncanny space. One cannot be fully safe in a multiplex and one definitely cannot feel at home at one's home. A multiplex, therefore, transforms into uncanny space and an integral part of a ghostly city. It is also a past intervening into the present, disrupting what would otherwise, perhaps, be the serenity of forgetfulness. Dead history and, literally, the dead, the murdered, come back to haunt the living in the spectral presence of unruliness in a space impossible to be hyper-orderly. Neoliberalism strives for conceptual cleanliness, a sanitization of non-place, which is always stained by unruliness, an impossibility to realize a neoliberal utopia. Gated space may seem orderly on the inside, but the spectral presence of past and otherness reminds us constantly that this is only an illusion, as my analysis of *NH10* has demonstrated. One, perhaps, has to make peace with *past populations*, the specters, and co-habit the same space. A unique film in this case is *Bhooter Bhobishyat* (Anik Dutta, 2012), a Bengali film focusing on the hard life of ghosts in contemporary Kolkata, a city in which, due to urban development and demolition of old buildings, the spaces where ghosts can dwell in peace are disappearing; there are less and less haunted houses. This, however, does not negate the haunting as a subversive act. Only that spatial implosion brings the ghosts and the living close together, and they have to learn to live side by side. As de Certeau writes, "the wordless histories of walking, dress, housing, or cooking shape neighborhoods on behalf of absences; they trace out memories that no longer have a place…. Such is the 'work' of urban narratives as well. To the visible city they add those 'invisible cities' about which Calvino wrote" (de Certeau 1998, 142). And such is the "work" of cinematic urban narratives of new Hindi cinema: they re-populate the urban map, the one that's visible, with the "invisible" cities of a not-so distant past.

Marc Augé (2008) calls highways, shopping malls, airport lounges and other similar transitory spaces non-places—places not yet produced as social spaces; places *impossible* to produce into social spaces. Such non-places are the heterotopian emplacements of postmodernity. He distinguishes a non-place from a "conventional" anthropological place as a place "which cannot be defined as relational, or historical, or concerned with identity" (Augé 2008: 63). Such spaces do not integrate earlier places, as he claims, unlike Baudelairean modernity. Charles Baudelaire was critical of the transforming city and the uneasiness the new urban architecture was provoking. Augé, on the other hand, writes of what he terms supermodernity—a highly advanced and intensified process of spatial dislocation and de-connection, to use Deleuze's notion. Cinema does engage with such processes in various ways, often portraying individuals attempting to transform non-places into places of dwelling and, ultimately, into social spaces, either successfully or not. *Bhoot*, indeed, presents a radical view of the extreme *Unheimlichkeit*— where and what was supposed to be a place was, in fact, a non-place to begin with, and turns against the individuals attempting to destroy them. Haunting, therefore, is a subversive act integrating past and present, as well as a non-place and anthropological place. Ghostly city, therefore, is a failed neoliberal utopia, but at the same time, the only utopian present or future available, as total sanitization is a theoretical fallacy.

Reading cinematic manifestations of the uncanny, haunted space and, in the words of Edward Dimendberg (2004), seeing it and the built environment as mutually implicated in the construction of spatial anxieties or architectural uncanny is an important point of departure for the analysis of new Hindi cinema. Drawing upon Henri Lefebvre's theorization of abstract space, he terms the transformed space of late noir cinema as centrifugal, as opposed to the centripetal space of modernity. The former, according to him, "initiates novel perceptual and behavioral practices—new experiences of time, speed and distance—no less than new features of the everyday landscape" (Dimendberg 2004: 169). While Baudelairean modernity and early and late modern-urban transformations fueled the imagination of artists in the late 19th and early to mid-20th century and fostered the emergence of imagining the dark side of urban experience, similar processes occurred in the second-half of the 20th century—in dematerialized, transient, mediatized spaces of what Bauman (2000) termed liquid modernity, a space-time where solidity of modernity becomes fluid, transient and unstable. In this condition, and in the experience of transformation toward this condition, a new type of uncanny begins to emerge, this time relating to dromospheric experience and transforming perception, emergence of non-places, centrifugal spaces and similar emplacements that evoke, first and foremost, ghostliness as they are ungraspable, virtual and about to move on, to be deterritorialized in order to materialize as something else once again. Such urban space, which is seemingly always on the move, overhauls the spatial experience and sociality, and causes estrangement from the surroundings and a space where, in the words of Bauman, strangers meet strangers and remain strangers, as opposed to Richard Sennett's definition of a city as a space where strangers meet (in Bauman 2000: 94–5). Shaviro (2010: 35–64) illustrates this problem with his analysis of Assayas' *Boarding Gate* (2007) very well.[2] In such a liquid or post-urban environment, meeting is difficult if not impossible. Non-place is not about meeting or sociality; it is constructed for very clear economic ends. And it does not matter which space we take as an example. A shopping mall, a multiplex or a Starbucks café—all produce an aura of public space and a space of social interaction but, in reality, are spaces of consumption. Highways, flyovers and ring roads—embodiments of neoliberal urban India—do not need to mask themselves as anything else but simply be silent arteries, usually built slightly above the city and its lower-class neighborhoods, facilitating rapid movement and *arrival at a destination*, whatever it may be, be it work, home, shopping mall or airport. The early 21st-century Indian city transforms from a space where *strangers meet strangers* into a space where strangers do not meet, where they should not meet. A flyover as part of transport infrastructure of the late 20th-century Indian city, in itself, has become a chronotope so often evoked in cinema and is designed to prevent any meeting; it diverts the bodies of city dwellers above and beyond the neighborhoods that need to be avoided due to urban congestion. Life would reach an impasse without flyovers. Moreover, one is more likely to experience encounters with spaces that are meant to be left behind and below. Flyovers

[2] Olivier Assayas engages with spectrality and capitalism far more directly in *Personal Shopper* (2016).

sanitize the urban space by creating lines of flight and, in the process, contribute to urban fragmentation and spatial deconnection. But such spaces that are mentally and often visually removed and left behind are always spectrally present, are lurking below and intervene into the sanitized space at any given moment, thereby negating the idea of order. We are no longer in a centripetal space of modern metropolis—a space of heavy and hard modernity, in Bauman's (2000) words. We are in a space that is centrifugal, that is liquid, a space "increasingly devoid of landmarks and centers" (Dimendberg 2004: 172). Or, in the words of Giorgio Agamben (2013: 474), larval spectrality comes to haunt the city where signs and signatures of the past have been made illegible and unreadable, and where cyphers are not so readily available.

In his interpretation, or rather refutation of Freud's concept of the uncanny, Mark Fisher (2016) takes up two notions which according to him are more appropriate terms: the weird and the eerie. Both the weird and the eerie, so deeply rooted in the gothic and in horror films, deal with the outside space. The home space rarely becomes eerie, though it can manifest some qualities of weirdness and be out of synch. The weird is closer to the notion of the uncanny in terms of blurred lines separating homely and unhomely (presence of strangeness in the familiar). Eerie is far deeply rooted in the outside space—a space that is emptied out, that is outside experience. But what happens when the home, the inside space, becomes devoid of the conventional markers of the homely? What happens when the home becomes eerie, which can be read as a radical manifestation of the uncanny? It happens precisely at the juncture when symbols become unreadable and space becomes deconnected.

Darr @ The Mall and *Phobia*

The uncanniness of such deconnected, unreadable spaces is evoked in another film that focuses on haunting—*Darr @ The Mall* (Pawan Kripalani, 2014). This film makes use of a shopping mall, transforming it into an uncanny space populated by ghosts killing the mall's visitors. The film offers a critique of neoliberalism woven with a horror story.

The film is shot almost entirely within the space of a shopping mall—
a fictional Amity Mall,[3] which is the largest mall in Asia and is set to
reopen. The other spaces in the film are only visible during flashbacks,
memories and dreams. However, employees notice strange events occurring; they see ghosts; they are assaulted; things move without human
intervention. The first scene of the film focuses on the killing of a security
guard at night; the first shot of the film is a desktop computer having
Edvard Munch's *The Scream of Nature* as a screensaver—a late 19th-
century expressionist work of art and an iconic modernist painting evoking fear and anxiety, an anxiety at the dawn of the brutal 20th century.

The main targets of the ghosts, as it appears, are not random visitors,
but the owners of the mall and their families. As we learn, the owners,
property developers, were trying to acquire, land on which the mall was
subsequently built, from an orphanage run by one Mother Madeline, a
nun. She was repeatedly refusing to sell the orphanage, and in the end,
it was set on fire, killing the nun and the children. It is they who become
ghosts haunting the mall and trying to avenge the destruction of their
home by what is probably one of the most emblematic examples of
neoliberal urbanism—property development, gentrification and shopping mall as key symbols of the post-liberalization age in India. The film,
thus, portrays the brutal modus operandi of real estate development,
and the ghosts are the Others haunting the upper-class self. The shopping mall as part of urban redevelopment destroys memories of the
past, the innocence and the intimate space of the childhood home. The
film's protagonist, a newly hired amnesiac security guard Shiv (Jimmy
Sheirgill), while investigating the haunted, uncanny spaces of the mall,
recovers from amnesia and remembers that he, in fact, is not Shiv, but
Ajay, and was one of the children living in the orphanage and the only
survivor of the brutality that destroyed his home. At the end of the
film, he screams at one of the owners and accuses him of destroying his
childhood, his home and killing his mother (the nun). The film can be
seen as a metaphor and a critique of urban development and shopping

---

[3] A tribute to the horror classic *The Amityville Horror* (Stuart Rosenberg,
1979).

mall culture, but at the same time, in its materiality, it constructs a space of a mall as the embodiment of neoliberal newness, which is gradually ruined by the return of the repressed, by the resurrection of the past. The erasure of history and installation of a space of consumption literally on the ashes of history demonstrates well how a non-place, a place that is not anthropological, is forged by attempting to cut off a centrifugal space from the historical time of a metropolis. But the space is stained by time, and the project of order, cleanliness and safe consumption is impossible. Shiv/Ajay's amnesia and the fact that he was a witness of the atrocity (that he has no memory of), which led to the erection of the non-place illustrate well how neoliberal capital attempts to transform space by violence and forgetting. Augé (2008: 63) remarks that the non-places are not relational or historical, and are not concerned with identity. I think the "concern with identity" is more crucial than that, because it is identity that gets transformed in such spaces—deterritorialized and reterritorialized, deconstructed and reassembled, always as something else, always different, producing the consumer's imaginary "global" identity. Acknowledging identity's relevance, he further states that "place and non-place are rather like opposed polarities: the first is never completely erased, the second never totally completed; they are like palimpsests on which the scrambled game of identity is ceaselessly rewritten" (Augé 2008: 64).

Darr @ The Mall juxtaposes two places: one historical or anthropological—an orphanage, which is never completely erased and is spectrally present, transforming the non-place into a ghostly space. The other—non-historical and non-anthropological—a shopping mall. Opposing spaces are also made distinct by the individuals populating them. There are two types of children in the film: the murdered children of the orphanage/past and the children of the present, a generation that is portrayed as ignorant of anything outside the circuits of mass consumption and "being-world-class", and in the process, are harshly punished by the murdered past, which haunts the present. But the past–present divide that the ghost necessarily represents is difficult to brush aside, and the "haunting" films, no matter how evocative they are, are unable to blur the past–present divide, except *Phobia* (Pawan

Kripalani, 2016), to which I shall turn shortly. For other attempts, one has to look elsewhere, into different kinds of films, like *Raaz 3* (Vikram Bhatt, 2012), which has nothing to do with haunting, but with the existence of a parallel dark universe, which acts as another layer of reality, where demons that possess the living dwell.

Going back to the shopping mall, or a temple of consumption as George Ritzer (2001) has called it, it is important to emphasize that this space is vital both for the process of mass consumption and the production of sameness. Malls essentially resemble one another, with small modifications everywhere in the world. A shopping mall is a heterotopia, insofar as it creates the illusion of a festival, a peculiar type of commodity worship in a temple of consumption. It is a place that pretends to be an *elsewhere* place, and it is always constructed and mediated as something else. In his study on brands, Arvidsson (2005: 78) talks about branded ambience and the "e-factor" as part of the strategy for how a shopping mall functions. Malls offer integrated entertainment (actual shopping and eating, but also virtual, imaginary travels in cinematic space, since many of them have multiplex cinemas), as well as shopping among similarly minded happy consumers. At the same time, keeping in mind the postcolonial metropolis, such a space excludes everything that might disturb the ambience of experience, such as subalternity, or lower social classes who do not have the means to consume in this way, but would perhaps like to stroll around and engage in window shopping. This space is emic space, a sanitized space that excludes otherness (Bauman 2000: 98–104). Going through such space is like traveling; it is like a voyage into the unreal, into a fantasy where you are among others like you. Bauman (2000: 98) states that "to go for such a trip is like being transported to another world, rather than witnessing the wondrous transubstantiation of the familiar one. The temple of consumption … may be in the city …, but is not a part of it; not the ordinary world temporarily transmogrified, but a 'completely other' world".

This is an important observation, which is similar to how Augé explains a non-place. In this other world, otherness can be both excluded and consumed. This is a space that acts as a closed circuit.

It has clearly defined entry and exit points, and it imposes a certain manner of worshipping, walking, observing and shopping. Describing a shopping mall, Scott Lash and Celia Lury state that "the physical environment is the setting for immersion in a highly mediated brand experience; very concretely, it is the *installation of sensation*" (Lash and Lury 2007: 7, emphasis mine). This is where forging a sensation produces lack; it is an installation not dissimilar to an artistic one. Production of lack is art and is being done by erecting spectacular heterotopian spaces in which we must desire or in which we are *interpellated* to desire, in an Althusserian sense of the term (Althusser 1971). However, many of these spaces manage to camouflage themselves as open spaces, that is, spaces of difference—but this difference is only branded difference, a commodified potentiality of any-space-whatever and an alternative that signifies the mainstream. In *Darr @ The Mall*, the Other finds its way into the emic space as a ghost and destroys what was supposed to be an "installation of sensation" and a pleasant shopping experience from within. A different kind of assault on a shopping mall as an exclusive and excluding space can be seen in *Mumbai Meri Jaan* (Nishikant Kamat, 2008). Thomas (Irrfan Khan), one of the characters in the film, is poor and cannot enjoy the shopping mall culture in any conventional manner. But he is a desiring consumer without the means to consume due to his poverty. He frequents a shopping mall, especially a perfume shop, in order to just spray some imported designer fragrance from a tester onto himself. One day, he comes with his wife and daughter. His wife struggles to get onto the escalator; clearly, she is not familiar with it, unlike those who frequent the mall. The space is new for her. They go into a perfume shop and attempt to consume in the way Thomas always does—by spraying some fragrance onto themselves for free. A shop assistant, upon seeing them, remarks to his colleague: "He comes here all the time, and now he brought all his family with him." Neatly groomed and smartly dressed, the shop assistant confronts Thomas, the security is called and the family of desiring consumers is thrown out of the shopping mall. For Thomas, this is an unbearable insult. His family is suddenly produced as the Other, as an unwanted element in a space in which it cannot participate in the shopping experience as is expected from them. Thomas is a bricoleur; he invents an alternative to commodity fetishism by consuming differently and by consuming an item—perfume—which can be considered a luxury commodity and a symbolic one, confirming one's status. Thus, Thomas resorts to a silent revolt against the shopping malls by calling them anonymously and announcing about a bomb on the premises (which, in each case, was never there). Then, from the distance, standing in a parking lot, he observes with great pleasure on his face the havoc he has unleashed on the consumers and the consuming process itself. His revolt against the neoliberal system comes from his frustration of not being accepted into it, not because he is fundamentally against it. He is a consumer denied participation in the spectacle of the shopping mall experience due to his status as an unwanted element. The mall as an emic space is constructed precisely in order to keep people like him outside. He constructs something that should be absent in a safe space of a mall—fear and panic. Just like ghosts in *Darr @ The Mall* or in *Bhoot*'s multiplex, he disrupts the safe space by uncovering a bitter truth: safety and serenity is only an illusion. He sets in motion a type of haunting that in many ways defines the early 21st-century metropolis—the haunting of terrorism, a fear that always lurks beneath the cozy surface of urban dwelling.

While majority of ghost stories focus on the repressed past coming to haunt the present, *Phobia* (Pawan Kripalani, 2016) is unique, because here it is the future that haunts the present, which is mistakenly perceived as the past. It is not so important what we inject into the substance of haunting; a phobic can inject anything depending on the unconscious, depending on his/her own history.

The slogan of the present times may be: "the only way is forward". Forwardness and newness mark the approach of neoliberal philosophy toward the past, the present and the future. Innovation, entrepreneurship and restlessness are haunting the neoliberal present. The past is commodified and history is appreciated as a tool in making profit (for example, beautification projects, sugarcoating of old towns for the purposes of tourist consumption, etc.). Such commodification of the material past recodes the symbols and makes them hard to decipher. The present is understood only as a transient space. The dream of the future dislocates the present and makes it transient, unstable. The dislocation of the present, if we were inclined to understand the present as a space of stability and homeliness, infuses it with a different type of haunting. It is not only the past that haunts the present, but also the future. Not only the dead haunt the living, but the *not-yet* haunts the present. For Derrida, the specter is not only something that was, but always what will be; it is also always the not-yet communicating with the present and the past. "Haunting is historical", he says, "but never *dated*, it is never docilely given a date in the chain of presents" (Derrida 2006: 4). Spivak (1995: 71), in her commentary on Derrida's ghosts, states that "because it coordinates the future in the past, the ghost is not only a revenant (a returner, the French for 'ghost'), but also an arrivant, one who arrives". Virilio, as I mentioned before, emphasizes the perpetual arrival as the marker to the dromological present, which makes the departure and the journey obsolete. Discontent with the present and the desire for immediate arrival can blur the present into a ghostly presence. The present is spectral because it is transient, and the future, a desire to arrive, in the imaginary, become a far more stable state of being. The ghost is *arrivant*, because we make it so by desiring, by forgetfulness, by inability to read the runes of the past and the present. This, in my view, is the ultimate manifestation of dromological pollution. It is always also the future that haunts the present of the neoliberal lifeworlds. It is the future, *the memory of futures* as the only stable though imagined reality, that destabilizes the present. Why might the future be mistaken for the past? Chronology breaks down in the haunted space-time, as does time itself. "Haunting", says Gordon (2008: xvi), "raises specters, and it alters the experience of being in time, the way we separate the past, the present, and the future". The blurred planes of past/future/present, in the way it dislocates time, in the way it displaces the present, in the way it deterritorializes linear life narrative, produces an agoraphobic condition, where one may be inclined to feel safe only in an enclosed space, a familiar space with homely everyday objects. The agoraphobic is a Bachelardian hero, incapable of accepting time out of joint, unable to imagine homeliness in the midst of imploding past/future/present vertigo. Such an agoraphobic self, always already othered, is a stain on the surface of the neoliberal forwardness vector and its esthetics of arrival and disappearance.

Mehak (Radhika Apte), an artist living in Mumbai, is suffering from agoraphobia. It is aggravated after a taxi driver sexually assaults her one night, on her way home. After the incident, she stays with her sister, who is tired of taking care of her and does not want her daughter to see the aunt's madness. She has regular sessions with a psychotherapist, who, interestingly, applies a virtual reality (VR) therapy. With the VR glasses on, Mehak finds herself in a shopping mall, of all the places, and she must overcome her agoraphobia by engaging in virtual shopping, although unsuccessfully: "No one will harm you here", the therapist states ambiguously, referring both to the unreality of the real and the shopping mall. And then there is the troubled relationship with her friend/boyfriend Shaan, who in the end, rents out an apartment for her. She is incapable of leaving the apartment due to her mental condition, cannot force herself to communicate with others in the building and is fully dependent on Shaan. Shortly after moving in, she starts seeing what she perceives as the ghost of a dying woman. After some inquiries, it comes to light that the previous inhabitant of the apartment, a young woman named Jiah, had a stormy relationship with a man living on the same floor and has disappeared. Mehak is convinced that the woman was murdered by the man and is haunting her. The film's climax is quite unusual: it appears that the "dying" woman is not the previous inhabitant, but Mehak herself, who got injured nearly fatally during a weird conflict with Shaan. It is not the dead from the past that is haunting Mehak, but her own future haunts the present and acts as a kind of premonition. *Phobia* is a radical film, because it nullifies the past by focusing squarely on the future, on the *arrivant* haunting the present. Mehak herself, her future self, is the arrivant; she haunts herself from the future. For her future becomes real when it is imagined as such. A possible future communicates with her and becomes the actual present, because Mehak accepts the future as something that has already happened. The film is highly unstable in its temporality and is circular as opposed to being linear or non-linear. It starts with an art exhibition, where Mehak is displaying her painting titled *Nazara*. The film ends with the same scene, and we are led to believe that she painted *Nazara* after the incident at the apartment. What about the event between the first and the last scenes of *Phobia*? This is open for interpretations. Thus, the central problem of the film is temporal dislocation.

Talaash

The films I discussed in this chapter, namely, *Raat, Bhoot, Darr @ The Mall* and *Phobia* deal with what can be termed as a "classic" dark space of horror cinema—the familiar, homely space transforming into an uncanny one. The remainder of this chapter will deal with a film that can be seen as "transitional", as bridging the gap in the different shades of the uncanny. *Talaash* (Reema Kagti, 2012)[4] bridges the gap between horror film and neo-noir film by embracing different layers of spectrality. In terms of narrative, it focuses on a police inquiry into a strange and fatal car accident that happened on Marine Drive in Mumbai at night. The one killed in the crash, the driver of the car, we are told, was a famous (and fictional) Bollywood actor Armaan Kapoor. A police officer investigating the case, Surjan 'Suri' Shekhawat (Aamir Khan), is a good example of the depressed and troubled male protagonist—one of the central features of classical noir. His wife Roshni (Rani Mukerji) is disturbed and depressed, as we learn later on, because of the death of their young son due to drowning. Suri blames himself, is insomniac, is neglecting his wife and spends his nights driving around the city. Many *pasts* haunt him—the past of his own life, of what he perceives as his fault that caused his son's death. His private past merges with the past of the dark city, the spectrality of the city's invisibles—the sex workers, the gangs and the underbelly of the city—an interior that perpetually haunts the exterior. The subalterns—migrants, sex workers, missing persons no one is looking for—can be seen as ghosts, different type of ghosts, living ghosts, as Esther Peeren (2014) puts it, but ones haunting from the shadows.

---

[4] Anurag Kashyap wrote additional dialogue for this film.

Suri's loneliness and depression in an uncanny home and his dete-
riorating relationship with his wife have brief interruptions by a quasi-
femme fatale, a sex worker Rosie/Simran (Kareena Kapoor). She is
helping Suri in solving the mysterious case, and as we later learn, she
is the mystery of the case, as she is helping Suri solve her own murder.
They always meet at night, either at a hotel, a restaurant or by the
sea. There is unspoken romanticism, a strange understanding of one
another. Rosie is a sex worker and as she herself says to Suri, people
like her "do not exist, therefore cannot vanish". She belongs to spectral
Mumbai; Mumbai that may often be refused to be seen, but manifests
in such films. She is the missing person no one is looking for. She was a
living ghost until she became the real one, haunting the present, forcing
the present to find her, to acknowledge her existence. Rosie represents
the underworld in a more profound sense as well. She is a ghost, and
only Suri can see her. He says to her in one scene, "You can get away
from this place, start a new life." She replies, "It is not that simple." One
cannot simply get away from the dark and uncanny city, and a new life
too, often, may be an unreachable object of desire in films like *Talaash*.
The dead actor Armaan and his friends were Rosie's clients. One night,
they were driving on the Marine Drive, and some of the men in the car
wanted to have sex with Rosie then and there. After a brief scuffle in
the car, the door suddenly opened and Rosie fell out. Instead of seeking
help, the men let Rosie die and have her buried in a secluded space.
From then on, Rosie haunts the exact spot where she died. She appears
to drivers, standing in the middle of the road, forcing them to drive off
into the ocean in an attempt to avoid the collision. The film, in contrast
to the majority of ghost stories, tries to reconcile the "real" world and
the peripheral, or parallel world of ghosts, whether real ones or the living ones. Rosie's revenge is different, as she pretends not to be a ghost
in the radical sense of the world. To Suri, she presents herself as a living
ghost of the urban underbelly. Suri, in turn, fails to distinguish between
the different types of spectrality, thereby confirming the elusive nature
of ghostliness and a thin line separating the dead and the marginal,
the outcasts. In addition to this, there is another "ghost" story in the
film. Suri's wife Roshni comes to believe that she can communicate

with their dead son through a medium. Suri, upon learning about this, at first rejects the idea as madness, but after realizing Rosie's ghostliness, becomes aware of the absent presence that constantly haunts the everyday life. The last scene is different from the darkness Mumbai is enveloped in throughout the film. Roshni and Suri are sitting by a lake, basking in the sunshine, holding each other. It is the same lake their son drowned in.

Thus we have arrived at a junction where the haunting of dark spaces gives way to a different type of terror, a different type of anxiety. Ghost as a metaphor dislocates the forgetfulness of the present and paves the way for uncanniness, which is there without any supernatural character—film noir, which is but another means of expression of the uncanny and of spectrality. In film noir, the darkness of the present haunts, but haunts differently.

4

FILM NOIR AND THE DARK SPACES OF NEW HINDI CINEMA

Anurag Kashyap's film *Bombay Velvet* (2015), based on Gyan Prakash's book *Mumbai Fables* (2010), is a fine example of nostalgia for the past. The past was violent and unruly but, at the same time, provided clarity, sureness and perhaps even intimacy as opposed to the rapidly shifting megalopolis of the early 21st century: a past that haunts. It is also an overt homage to film noir, a form that has greatly influenced not only Anurag Kashyap, one of the finest neo-noir film-makers in India but also new Hindi cinema in general. Such nostalgia for a late modernity vis-à-vis the dromospheric pollution, in the words of Virilio (2008: 64), of the present is nothing new. Nostalgic wanderings in the spaces of childhood by Bachelard as opposed to the spatial uncanny of classical noir and the annihilation of serene intimacy is a good example (Sobchack 1998). At the same time, it is nostalgia for a centripetal, centered city—a city before neoliberalism; before Bombay became Mumbai; before the post-liberalization turn transformed it into a "global city" populated by ahistorical non-places and strangers who never meet. Differences between *Bombay Velvet* and other works by Kashyap, most importantly *Ugly* and *Raman Raghav 2.0*, are striking. However, the most striking thing about the film is its construction of pastiche, of peculiar "pastness", in the words of Jameson (1991: 19–21), which manifests as a stylized image, where the "pastness" as style is evoked by, first and foremost, fashion.

This chapter explores another dimension of the urban uncanny and dark imagination by dealing with a cinematic form, which has become, if not dominant, then visible in most new Hindi films—film noir esthetics. The usage of film noir esthetics in India did not began in the post-liberalization period and can be observed in a wide range of films dating back to the 1950s, a decade when noir-ish cinema existed as a subgenre (Prasad 2000: 86). Overall, the history of noir in Hindi cinema can be divided into two distinct periods—before and after liberalization. If in the "before" period, the usage of such esthetics was scarce and was limited only to a handful of films spanning the decades, after the liberalization, film noir became a common feature. Some historically important films containing noir elements include *Mr. and Mrs. 55* (Guru Dutt, 1955), *C.I.D.* (Raj Khosla, 1956), *Bees Saal Baad* (Biren Nag, 1962), *Kohraa* (Biren Nag, 1964), and also *Mahal* (Kamal Amrohi, 1949), *Madhumati* (Bimal Roy, 1958) and *Woh Kaun Thi?* (Raj Khosla, 1964), although the last three can be seen as more mystery than noir films. These films do not constitute any tendency, contrary to the emergence of post-liberalization noir in the 1990s, especially in the films by Ram Gopal Varma. In this book, I am not concerned with the overall history of film noir in Hindi cinema, but with a specific period and specific themes the films evoke; themes that, broadly speaking, belong and were invented, cinematically, by film noir in Hollywood and its predecessors in European cinemas. Film noir historically is a cinema of the end of modernity; a cinema of transformation; a cinema of a city with all its uncanniness, alienation and phobias. An unselfconscious cinema reflecting a shifting cultural and economic landscape and the transformations of cultural sensibilities. In order to demonstrate how film noir contributes to imagining neoliberal India, I shall continue with locating the problem of cinematic anxiety and will explore some key films in the post-liberalization period containing noir elements.

The Roots of Noir Anxiety

Film noir is notoriously hard to define, and different film scholars produce varied views on the phenomena (Oliver and Trigo 2002; Naremore 2008; Dixon 2009; Osteen 2013). Film noir as a quintessential film form reflecting urban uncanny emerged in Hollywood in the early 1940s and lasted till the late 1950s, although the name to this bleak and violent cinematic imagination was given by the French film critics, Nino Frank most prominently, who coined the term in 1946. Such films, detective stories, provided the language required to express far deeper tensions in the society. Some of the central conventions of film noir include a menacing city as a setting; a troubled private detective, often traumatized, heavily drinking, cynical, as the protagonist, who is hired to solve a crime; and a woman posing a threat to the male hero—what came to be known as femme fatale, and can be observed in some of the classical examples like *The Maltese Falcon* (John Huston, 1941), *The Woman in The Window* (Fritz Lang, 1944), *Double Indemnity* (Billy Wilder, 1944), *Laura* (Otto Preminger, 1944), *The Postman Always Rings Twice* (Tay Garnett, 1946), *The Big Sleep* (Howard Hawks, 1946), *They Live by Night* (Nicholas Ray, 1948), *Sunset Boulevard* (Billy Wilder, 1950), among others.

Noir did not appear in vacuum and was heavily influenced, from the point of view of cinema and literature, by American "hardboiled" crime fiction, especially by works of Raymond Chandler and Dashiell Hammett; French pre-war realist cinema, sometimes called poetic realism or even proto-noir (for example, *La Bête Humaine* (Jean Renoir, 1938) and *Pépé le Moko* (Julien Duvivier, 1937)); and Weimar cinema (for example, *M* (Fritz Lang, 1931)). The latter cinema had a profound esthetic impact, as many of the "pioneers" of Hollywood's film noir were German film-makers like Fritz Lang, Billy Wilder, Otto Preminger, Robert Siodmak, among others, who fled to the United States in the 1930s, following Hitler's seizing of power. The emerging film noir in the 1940s retained many cinematic conventions of German expressionist cinema, now deeply associated with classical noir, like low-key and chiaroscuro lighting and feelings of anxiety and paranoia, although they hybridized it with Hollywood filmic conventions (Koepnick 2002; Kaes 2003). Being exiles and strangers, the émigré directors and film technicians managed to comprehend American political realities "from outside", and produce a critical, dark portrayal of lives in the cities of the time. Anton Kaes (2003: 57) claims that their exilic experience, loss of home and intellectual homelessness also had an impact on the style of film noir.

A canonical interpretation of noir involves several interrelated problems—rapidly changing social fabric and social relation in the United States during World War II and the years after, male response to "crisis of masculinity" in the face of shifting gender balance, transforming and expanding cities, rise of fear during the initial years of the Cold War and the fear of nuclear annihilation. Paradoxically, the post-War period is usually regarded as the "Golden Age" of the United States, in which it became one of the two most powerful and richest countries in the world. Still, noir presents a very different mental map of the United States: one filled with anxiety, uncertainty, uncanny spaces, lonely men fearing women and trying to negotiate newness—spatial, sexual and racial. At the center of noir always is a dark and menacing, dehumanizing city. According to many readings, the cynical male protagonist in these films represents an average American man who went to war, and came back to see his country transformed, his unquestionable patriarchal white male authority challenged by women in the public space, by increasing presence of African Americans (or Others), Latin Americans, etc. Another important point in understanding noir anxiety is the city. Noir is a city cinema and usually shows the dark side of urban living, often of Los Angeles, and the crime, spiritual poverty and degradation that, if we can interpret by reading these films, plague a modern American city. Thus, the frustration, though never explicit in these films, comes from the changing or changed social, political and cultural fabric of society: the tensions of decades following the Great Depression, the war and the post-War years of fear and uncertainty—massive and alienating growth of the cities, fear of another economic crisis, the start of the Cold War and the fear of the Other in the form of Communism. All these tensions bled into film noir. The transformation, whatever it may be, is painful and is the source of trauma, which has to be in some way channeled out, be it by violence and hypermasculinity, of which I shall talk in the last chapter, or by artistic expressions.

Looking at film noir from a philosophical angle and extending my arguments laid out in the previous chapter, this film form had also produced a phobic space and offered the quintessential "paranoiac imagination". It was a "cinema of paranoia, of doubt and fear and uncertainty" (Dixon 2009: 1). Slavoj Žižek (2007: 173) argues that "the paranoia of the *noir* universe is primarily visual, based upon the suspicion that our vision of reality is always already distorted by some invisible frame behind our backs". Paranoia in the noir universe relates to the problematizing of interior and exterior, and the partial collapse of clearly defined boundaries. This can be understood in several ways. Noir as a film form itself escapes compartmentalization and crosses the boundaries of genres. Such nomadic esthetic movement collapses clear-cut understanding of a genre. Could this be understood as a kind of empty signifier? Perhaps, but emptiness in this case is filled with phenomena. Secondly, paranoia relates to the social context of noir, where noir itself is a signifier of transformations far away from cinema. Hybridizing space and the emergence of "thirdness", to borrow Homi Bhabha's term, as a sociocultural mélange is in itself ungraspable and, usually, a source of paranoia. Clearly defined mental spaces in our case may include a middle-class social space and a lower-class one, a separation between urban center and rural periphery. Such clear boundaries on the one hand are becoming meaningless in the age of globalization; on the other, the boundaries of interior/exterior are always being reinforced, as this is one of the key elements of modernity. The binary, of course is held together by Foucauldian power relations. Such power relations are not difficult to figure out; they relate to neoliberalism and new urban middle classes and their objects of desire—desires for safety, security, serenity. Such a state of mind can be nothing less than neurotic, as boundaries belong more to the world of desire without fulfillment, that is, to the order of the Real than reality. Third, paranoia, as Žižek demonstrates, is also visual. He discusses the work of Edward Hopper, a painter and an erstwhile cover illustrator of noir detective novels, arguing that "his paintings enforce the idea of spaces and elements beyond the limits of the scene itself" (Žižek 2007: 174). What's important in such spatial representation is the play between *champs* and *hors-champs*, and their reference to an "external, absent supplement" (Žižek 2007: 174). Hopper simultaneously portrays interior and exterior. In this sense, the paranoiac object lies outside the field of vision, that is, hors-champs. Writing on paranoia, Victor Burgin (1991: 23) states:

> In an image saturated environment which increasingly resembles the interior space of subjective fantasy turned inside out, the very subject-object distinction begins to break down, and *the subject comes apart in the space of its own making.* As Terry Eagleton has written, the postmodern subject is one "whose body has been scattered to the winds, as so many bits and pieces of reified technique, appetite, mechanical operation or reflex of desire". Such fragmentation, decentering and loss of subject-object boundaries, is characteristic of paranoia. (emphasis mine)

Oliver and Trigo (2002: xiv) in their study of film noir also claim that interpreting noir only as a response to social transformation is reductive. They are "locating the anxiety of noir at the heart of identity formation itself". Furthermore, they claim that "by interpreting film noir as a type of Freudian dream-work marked by condensations and displacements of unconscious desires and fears, we begin to see some of the ways in which anxieties over borders operate as a return of the repressed and as defense mechanisms in the service of identity" (Oliver and Trigo 2002: xv).

This is precisely the point. Anxiety over the border that is collapsing, making the interior/exterior boundary porous so that the undecidables, to use Derrida's notion, or nomads to use Deleuze and Guattari's, can easily cross over and move in unpredictable and spontaneous ways.

Film noir has traveled a long way since its prime in post-War United States and it became a transnational phenomenon influencing filmmakers around the world (Desser 2003). As a film form evoking dark mental spaces and the uncanny materiality of social transformation, it has become a film form embodying the dark side of life in an age of rapid social change that is in opposition to "official" history—often of prosperity, good life, safety and material comforts. Sobchack (1998) in her reading of film noir juxtaposes the "official" American post-War history and uneasiness provoked by the social and spatial transformations. The tendency of bleakness vis-à-vis the "official" story in general can be observed in various cinemas immediately after the World War II, for example, Akira Kurosawa's post-War noir *Stray Dog* (1949) and his bleak crime films like *Drunken Angel* (1948) or *The Bad Sleep Well* (1960); Italian neorealism and the films of Luchino Visconti, Roberto Rossellini, Vittorio De Sica; and also the "late neorealism" of Michelangelo Antonioni in *La Notte* (1961) or *L'Eclisse* (1962), expressing the alienating urban change. In short, not so much film noir, but bleakness and some of the noir elements have become global. Looking at global social, political and cultural transformations immediately following World War II, dark cinema as a means to express anxiety over the present and the future should not be a surprise. Darkness can be considered as a tendency, one that became more spurious with time and resurrected again as neo-noir—a film form very different from the classic noir—highly rhizomatic, but always containing the bleakness and claustrophobia of modern (or postmodern) life.

After the noir's classical period in the mid-20th century, the elements of noir remained as part of cinematic imagination, and as Naremore (2008: 2) argues, "film noir has become one of the dominant intellectual categories of the late twentieth century, operating across the entire cultural arena of art, popular memory, and criticism".

Film noir itself, if we speak of Hollywood cinema, has always acted more like a rhizome, to use Deleuze and Guattari's (2004) term, but especially so if we look at neo-noir cinema. Neo-noir is a form that emerged in the 1970s, after the classical noir period, and it usually appropriates only some elements of the noir—crime, bleakness, often a male protagonist who is either a private detective or a police officer, a criminal or just a person experiencing unhomeliness in its different forms. The beginnings of neo-noir are in nostalgia for the past, longing for a lost "golden age"—ironically, the American "golden age" was imagined as the 1930s—in the tumultuous time following the Great Depression, just before the war. Such a view of the past provides an illusionary stability of identity and spatial comfort; it is a pre-mediatized space that can be comprehended. And indeed, such is a function of nostalgic, retrospective neo-noir, which looks at the past with longing, ignoring the fact that the past may have been as brutal and oppressive as the present. Looking back and imagining the spaces of the past with nostalgia by adopting the style of film noir, as the present becomes too difficult to bear, can be traced to Roman Polanski's *Chinatown* (1974), often perceived as the first neo-noir film that emerged after a long absence of noir sensibility in Hollywood. The 1970s was a troubled period in US history, a time when one wanted to look back at what was perceived as the "golden age" of 20th-century America—1930s. The emergence of neo-noir in the 1970s can also be related to the shifts in the sociopolitical fabric of the time: the cynical post-Kennedy era, the rise of discontent with the state following the Vietnam War, the civil rights movement, the ongoing Cold War and, most importantly, the first experiments with neoliberal economic policies, initially in Chile following the US-sponsored coup d'etat in 1973, before they became the cornerstone economic policies in the 1980s. It is not surprising, thus, that during the troubled times, a dark imagination started proliferating once again. Also, it is not surprising that the film I mentioned at the beginning of this chapter, *Bombay Velvet*, is set in the 1960s—a decade before the Emergency and the crisis of Indian democracy, before the rise of Naxalism, before the disillusionment with the developmentalist postcolonial state, before the arrival of a cynical anti-hero in the form of Amitabh Bachchan's "angry young man" to the screens to fight for a place under the sun in a city.

Neo-noir is a self-conscious cinema; it purposefully adopts a certain style. It is far more philosophically pervasive and pensive, and can be understood as a philosophy of noir (Gilmore 2007). According to Dimendberg (2004: 255), "the end of film noir also coincides, and not fortuitously, with the end of the metropolis of classical modernity, the centered city of immediately recognizable and recognized spaces". Noir's nostalgia is far more unconscious; by representing alienation, loneliness and the uncanny city of late modernity, noir longs for a "golden age" that was seemingly less complex, and the identities in which were far more fixed and stable.

Hindi neo-noir, as I shall demonstrate shortly, is itself a symptom of far more profound anxieties dating back to the 1980s and, later, to the neoliberalization of the 1990s. The spaces of this cinema are filled with such undecidables, whether we see them as individuals or simply as esthetics moving away from cinematic representation into the field of (paranoiac) *unrepresentability*, or, what I would call, following Virilio (2008), dromological esthetics. Shaviro (2010: 42), in his analysis of post-cinematic esthetics, invokes Deleuze's (2005) notion of any-space-whatever, which is not dissimilar to Marc Augé's (2008) non-places that I discussed earlier. Such spaces are indeterminate; movements through such spaces are without any destination. Non-existence of destination to which we should arrive constructs a space of perpetual movement, but such positive position negates the powerful impulses of neoliberal reason to forge the destination as an object of desire. Among the sources of paranoia of neo-noir is not an existential fear that the destination does not exist (that is, the object of desire does not exist), but of precisely the opposite: deep inside, we know that the destination is there, but we do not yet know what that may be. In a rapidly transforming neoliberal space, the object of desire undergoes transformation itself, becoming ungraspable, even if for a brief moment. In my opinion, Deleuze's as well as Shaviro's positions that I discussed earlier negate the existence of desire, and one cannnot negate desire in the times of neoliberal subjectivity.

Dark Cinematic Spaces and Urban India in the 21st Century

In Hindi cinema, the emergence of noir sensibility as a tendency can be traced to the late 1980s, a time, as I mentioned many times, of several interrelated social, political and cultural transformations—the gradual adoption of neoliberalism and the rise of the Hindu Right. The emergence in India must be understood as a part of the pattern of "global noir". Similar responses in the 1990s could be seen in Hong Kong, Latin America, United States and Europe. It was the changing landscape on multiple levels that triggered a slow emergence of such cinematic imagination. At first, throughout the 1990s, it was a more limited phenomenon, often associated with the films (directed and produced) by Ram Gopal Varma, a film-maker who at that time became a mentor to several young and aspiring men who would become important new Hindi cinema representatives, like Anurag Kashyap and Sriram Raghavan.

Some of the most important works of that time include *Siva* (Ram Gopal Varma, 1989 [Telugu version]), *Parinda* (Vidhu Vinod Chopra, 1989), *Raakh* (Aditya Bhattacharya, 1989), culminating with Varma's classic Bombay gangster film *Satya* (1998). Writing on *Parinda*, one of the first films to evoke such dark imagination, Ranjani Mazumdar (2002: 71) states that Bombay in this film

> is fragmented into *dark, morbid spaces* with all the characters framed within a light and shadow zone. Rarely in the film do we see a riot or spectacular display of colour. There is a *peculiar obsession for the night, for darkly lit interior spaces* that are fragmented as against the panoramic vision one usually gets in Hindi cinema. (emphasis mine)

Indeed, obsession with dark spaces, the night and suffocating interiors is what marks the noir imaginary, but more than that, it signifies a transforming perception of the urban life as having a peculiar heart of darkness at its core. To make no mistake, this city is very different from the "angry" city of the 1970s in *Zanjeer* (Prakash Mehra, 1973) or *Deewar* (Yash Chopra, 1975)—a city that was still embedded in pre-neoliberal Nehruvian developmentalism. Tracing the genealogy of the cinematic city, Ravi Vasudevan (2010: 313) states:

> From the 1950s onwards, Bombay popular cinema has taken crime as a key thematic, generic form, and mode of urban representation and experience. While these earlier forays used criminality to dramatize social injustice, and as metaphoric narrative for situations of illegitimacy and social exclusion, the contemporary cinema from the mid-1970s develops a different symbolic narrative of crime.

It has to be emphasized that 1970s was the time of discontent, of the rise of Naxalism in West Bengal, political and social tensions and the Emergency. On the cinematic front, it was the time when the New Wave emerged. While auteurs like Shyam Benegal focused on rural India, the bleak city dominated the imagination of independent, critical cinema of that time, from works like Mrinal Sen's *Calcutta 71* (1971) and Ritwik Ghatak's *Jukti, Takko Aar Gappo* (1977) to Govind Nihalani's *Ardh Satya* (1983) and Saeed Akhtar Mirza's *Albert Pinto ko Gussa Kyon Ata Hai* (1980) and *Salim Langde Pe Mat Ro* (1989), among many others. But, as Vasudevan (2010: 313) rightly notes, film-makers at that time were more preoccupied with questions of social justice as well as communal tensions. The late 1980s saw a different type of darkness emerging—less concrete and more psychological, and definitely more obsessive.

Obsessions with darkness must be contextualized vis-à-vis the emerging material culture of "unbearable lightness": gentrified, estheti-cized neoliberal culture and obsession with cleanliness of an orderly global space. Material space is as important as a mental or metaphorical one—its impact on social relations as well as on imagination, and also, the effect of material space on cinema.

A large section of new Hindi cinematic imaginary owes a lot to the film noir genre and the adoption of noir esthetic style can be found in many films, ranging from more popular, commercial new Hindi cinema, to more indie examples. Among the plethora of film-makers, Anurag Kashyap stands out as a kind of "godfather" of Hindi neo-noir and dirty realism. His films are often bleak, violent, offer little hope or resolution, present a crisis of the individuals and what may be called the dark side of life. His protagonists are usually lonely neurotic men dwelling in the shadowlands of neoliberal and mostly urban India. Apart from Kashyap's, many more films evoke the noir style, like *Jism* (Amit Saxena, 2003), *Talaash* (Reema Kagti, 2012), *Manorama Six Feet Under* (Navdeep Singh, 2007), *Shaitan* (Bejoy Nambiar, 2011), *Kahaani* (Sujoy Ghosh, 2012), *Kaminey* (Vishal Bhardwaj, 2009), *CityLights* (Hansal Mehta, 2014), Sriram Raghavan's *Ek Hasina Thi* (2004) and *Badlapur* (2015), among many others.

In discussing several films strongly evoking the new esthetic form, Ranjani Mazumdar (2010: 153–4) states that these films

introduce formal innovations that actively disturb and haunt globaliza-tion's visual culture of brightness to sculpt an alternative language of space that is dark, melancholic, and dystopic. This is a cinema that exists on the periphery of Bombay's cinematic excess where the "blindness" generated by habitual cultures of seeing is rearranged to make the spectator see what has not been seen before.

Darkness, melancholy and dystopia, or a derailed neoliberal utopia, as well as hybrid urban culture and hybrid identity formation give an impulse to the rise of new esthetics negotiating marginality, the overlapping of light and darkness producing undecidable space, unmasking the "blindness" of a spectator Mazumdar (2010: 154) refers to. Across the wide spectrum of Hindi cinema, many film-makers demonstrate interest in "dark space". Some films and film-makers on a more mainstream side could include Vishal Bhardwaj and his films like *Kaminey* (2009) or *7 Khoon Maaf* (2011), as well as the "Shakespearean trilogy"—*Maqbool* (2003), *Omkara* (2006) and *Haider* (2014);[1] Tigmanshu Dhulia and his *Shagird* (2011), as well as his mofussil films *Saheb Biwi aur Gangster* (2011) and *Saheb Biwi aur Gangster Returns* (2013). But far more interesting appropriations and transforming negotiations are taking place further away from mainstream Hindi cinema in cinema that shies away from the popular form and incorporates far more "darkness and dirt" than the former. The films I shall refer to do treat space "as a bad object", as Mazumdar (2010: 156) claimed. The collapsing nature of binaries of self and Other, inside and outside, demands to investigate the spatial negativity of these films more closely. Jameson (1996: 156), in a different context, claims that "the city ... becomes one immense amorphous unrepresentable container". Speaking of city as such a "container", it is perhaps even worth mentioning, outside cinema, dark and disturbing novels by Raj Kamal Jha that are trying to negotiate the "global" India, urban growth and its impact on people's lives, like *If You are Afraid of Heights* (2003) and *She Will Build Him a City* (2015). Both novels can be understood as dirty realist, with a strong postmodern vertigo-like narrative structure, at times evoking a stream of consciousness, which was not very common in American dark realist novels of the 1970s and 1980s. In cinema, especially in films set in the

---

[1] Though the latter two are not set in urban areas.

cities, such unrepresentability, mapping and "presentation" instead of "representation" becomes more of a norm than exception, especially in films outside the mainstream. Incapability to smoothly negotiate the speed of transforming affect translates into the cinematic esthetics of disappearance (Virilio 2009). This "disappearance" gives birth to the uncanny; to the feeling of transitory spaces, of life fleeting by, as if we were looking at a blurred video shot from a moving car.

Space and Dark Cinematic Philosophy

Bhaskar Mukhopadhyay (2012: 6), in discussing the production and the performativity of space, claims that "the map is not the territory and the space of the world always exceeds its mimetic representation and, in that sense, it must be thought as unrepresentable". Drawing upon Doreen Massey, he sees production (and transformation) of space as manifestation of unrepresentability freeing the subject from "the shackles of Cartesian-Kantian representational thinking" (Mukhopadhyay 2012: 22). Deleuze (2005: 109) calls such space "any-space-whatever". He claims that such space "is a space of virtual conjunction, grasped as pure locus of the possible. What in fact manifests the instability, the heterogeneity, the absence of link of such a space, is a richness in potentials or singularities" (Deleuze 2005: 109). Movement through such space is a movement without arriving at a destination. Neo-noir and dirty realist tendencies within the new Hindi cinema, being cinema of the transformational, transient period, in terms of offering no resolution and being simply particles of lifeworlds, present a spatial movement without arrival, as it is not (yet) clear what the destination should be. This is a manifestation of post-cinematic esthetics in Hindi cinema—a social commentary deprived of social commentary; politics without the political (Shaviro 2016). Such *no-arrival* esthetics as there no longer is a destination offers a transformed type of affect, a very different sensibility as "it does offer us a kind of satisfaction and relief, by telling us that we have finally hit bottom, finally realized the worst" (Shaviro 2015: 13). Such an anti-realist position calls into question representation as such, and demands evaluation of the unrepresentability of the contemporary, neoliberal lifeworlds. Unrepresentability, as Jameson (1991: 51–3) called it, transforms mimesis itself. Transformational space is haptic, but due to speed, the perception of phenomena transforms. This calls for new esthetics without a destination. Lack of destination, a cinematic departure without arrival and a constant nomadic movement may explain the inability of different film critics and scholars to grasp dirty realism, and hence call it meaningless. This is a position very similar to the one Jameson had with postmodernism as "waning of affect" (Jameson 1991: 55 76).

Homi K. Bhabha provides a critique of Jameson's problem of unrepresentability. He claims that "what must be mapped as a new international space of discontinuous historical realities is, in fact, the problem of signifying the interstitial passages and processes of cultural difference that are inscribed in the 'in-between', in the temporal break-up that weaves the 'global' text" (Bhabha 2004: 217). I would argue that new Hindi cinema, especially neo-noir, are, by and large, texts of cultural difference, and essentially attempts at "global" writing in times of cultural change. It is precisely the thirdness of culture's in-between that the films articulate that makes it unrepresentable. In general, the disappearance of certain signifiers (for example, item numbers) from new Hindi cinema can be understood as cultural hybridization and "thirding". At the same time, we must keep in mind that the cultural difference is part of a problem feeding the new film form. Foreignness has to be understood both as a negotiation of globality and articulation of sociocultural foreignness of the *local* in terms of internal Others haunting the upper-middle-class self. Jameson's problem, and Bhabha elaborates on this, is the inability to move beyond the "binary dialectic of inside and outside" (Bhabha 2004: 222), as well as to acknowledge that when it comes to spatial separation at the moment of cultural encounter, it is not the separation that is a crucial phenomenon, but an interstice that opens up, a new space in-between the binary dialectics of inside/outside and self/Other—a space of ambivalent cultural newness.

For Jameson, as well as for many functioning within the Eurocentric philosophical tradition, there has to be a clearly demarcated interior and exterior, self and Other, base and superstructure, while in reality, the negotiation in-between thins the neat boundaries by making them porous for the nomadic crossings. The porosity is one of the sources of anxiety, as it means instability and undecidability. Bhabha (2004: 221) writes:

> Jameson attempts, in a suggestive move, to turn the schizophrenic social imaginary of the postmodern subject into a crisis in the collective ontology of the group faced with the sheer "number" of demographic pluralism. The perceptual (and cognitive) anxiety that accompanies the loss of "infrastructural" mapping becomes exacerbated in the postmodern city, where both Raymond Williams's "knowable community" and Benedict Anderson's "imagined community" have been altered by mass migration and settlement.

Bhabha goes on to critique Jameson's focus on social class, a category through which any kind of mobilization can be mediated. Taking into consideration India and new Indian *middle classness* as a dream to build a *postmodern city*, class and caste differences must be taken into account as one of the important sources of *schizophrenic social imaginary* of the *new global bourgeoisie*. Bhabha is right, however, in emphasizing the transformation in Williams's and Anderson's ideas on community. Migration does alter them, and migration in this sense should be understood in several ways: a physical migration into the cities from the periphery, the effect of upper-class migration into the Global North and the two-way migrations of the imaginary. In the latter case, the concepts, forms and lifestyles baptized as "global" migrate, merging with local cultural symbols and producing new hybrid cultural symbols and practices. Such imaginary migration or symbolic migration transforms the cultural landscape and destabilizes and complicates the idea of locality. Such emergent newness can indeed cause anxiety for the "postmodern" subject and can be the source of the uncanny. Srivastava in his study on sexuality in contemporary urban India states the following, having in mind migration, and this also illustrates my own concerns:

> They are not merely migrants to the city, they are also migrants within it, located in spaces that are rapidly transforming, often hostile,

bewilderingly unfamiliar, out of reach and, depending upon how often they are "cleared" of urban slums and shanty towns, literally shifting beneath their feet. "Migrancy" here is then more than a change of place; it is the instability of space through which certain forms of unstable male subjectivities emerge. (Srivastava 2007: 140)

Srivastava refers to migrant laborers in Mumbai, who frequent sex clinics, but, importantly, emphasizes the multiplicity of meaning "migrancy" can have. It is a spatial instability out of which unstable and constantly shifting identities emerge. Instability in terms of space and identity can be understood as hybrid spaces and identities in-between—far too unstable to measure, enumerate and compartmental-ize. "Migrancy" is also the migration of the imaginary, the migration of cultural codes that are constantly rewritten, presenting us with a daunting, if not impossible, task of translating them into familiar lan-guage. Transforming cultural landscape is unrepresentable or beyond the uncomplex mimesis due to the instability of the third space, which goes beyond as well as against Eurocentric philosophy and Eurocentric imaginary of globalization. Film noir has often been called a transna-tional film form, given its roots in Weimar and French cinemas and their influence on Hollywood "cultural translations", and later esthetic migrations and transmogrifications globally, in Europe, Asia and Latin America. The unrepresentable global financial flows fueling the very foundations of globalization are translated into the cultural multiplicity of the dark "other side" of globalization, making noir the cinema of glo-balization, and reflecting similar concerns on the global scale—gentri-fication, increasing social exclusion and the rise of deconnected spaces.

Transforming global esthetic form can also be viewed as deterritori-alized form. Such form is indeed nomadic and rhizomatic as opposed to rooted realism with social messages and arrivals at a destination, whatever that destination might be. Such dromological esthetics, only without arrival or destination, is an event new Hindi cinema performs. Therefore, unrepresentability, mapping as opposed to mimesis, for me, means cinema without arrival, a dromospheric cinema, which is beyond representation in a phenomenological sense, as the phenomena is no longer (or not yet) graspable. What is left is not a representational

practice, but the labor of mapping. Such position may seem to be similar to Jean Baudrillard's, but in my view, his proposition that reality no
longer exists and is replaced by a map as hyperreality is far-fetched
(Baudrillard 1994: 1–2). Reality is just far less graspable by means of
representation, if we speak of art. What is effective is a process of presentation or mapping, where an artist is no longer (or, not so much)
concerned with representation, but with presentation and acts more
like a nomadic cartographer than film-maker. Such a cinematic cartographer creates not representations, but events, and a cinematic map is
far more of an event than representation.

I would relate these questions with Mazumdar's rhizomatic perception of Bollywood noir and her understanding of at least some of
this flow as anti-realist (Mazumdar 2010: 156n16). More than other
Hindi films in the past, the new urban social imaginary is deterritorialized and relates more to the problem of mapping than representing.
The bleak elements of neo-noir serve the purpose well in evoking the
spatial collapse between the neat binaries of modernity and evolu-
tion into overlapping spaces filled with uncertainty, insecurity, fear
and violence. Such overlapping hybrid spaces of neoliberal India are
the homely spaces transformed into uncanny ones. Film does act as
a mental-mapping procedure of a territory, which is by all means not
hyperreal, as Baudrillard would have had it, but undecidable and filled
with ambivalent individuals trying to negotiate their new hybrid selves.
Disappointment, a spiraling into the bottom, but more often the feeling of the uncanny, and to some extent a 'stairway to hell', mark Hindi
cinema in the post-liberalization period.

Neo-noir imagination in particular can be seen as an existential
allegory of the transforming mental landscape or "psychoscape" of
urban middle-class India, and an attempt to map new realities, new
relationships in terms of class, caste and gender, as well as in terms of
spatial locations and dislocations. By the latter, I mean the complex
relationship between the urban metropolis and its periphery; between
new middle class and old middle class; between gated community and
urban slum. Metropolis/global city and a periphery are not necessarily
(or, usually not) geographical categories; they have to be understood as

mental territories, products of affective mapping where cinema plays an important role. Such mapping produces subjectivity of both the upper middle class and the subaltern Other.

Consumerism, spatial transformations and unconscious capitalist "re-education" of the masses into becoming consumers contributed to the rise of new esthetics and must be seen in the context of increasing upward mobility of the corporate classes and the proliferation of what Fernandes (2006: 34) calls "symbolic frames of identity": markers of neoliberal ontology like shopping malls, exclusive and closed spaces— closed in order to exclude the undesirables, the Other of the neoliberal self, that is—the lower classes, workers, the poor, the rural migrants. Signs of Indian "third worldness" were undesirable in this sense and had to be eliminated from the field of vision. Of course, an important feature and another symbol was the proliferation of gated communities, spaces of safety and serenity outside the "chaotic" negotiation of globality on the street. Inside, globality was desired and negotiated differently, by identifying oneself with the "global" far more intimately. But the proximity of the Other, the fact that the binary of outside/ inside is imaginary, that it is the overlapping space and overlapping identities were forming—this caused a great deal of anxiety. Or, in other words, we must refer to the presence of the uncanny. Indeed, neo-noir showcases the manifestation of the urban uncanny, which is the result of negotiation of globality and new cultural formations. Fixation on the middle class's Other in many of the Hindi neo-noir films is an attempt to negotiate newness. It also signifies the inability to accept the existence of the othered self or ontological undecidability. Decidability, clarity, clearly defined spaces of home and its periphery— the urban uncanny emerges from the unreachability of these peculiar objects of desire. It emerges from the tension of undecidability on the one hand and from the externalized Real as an (unreachable) object of desire, on the other. Herein lies the entry into understanding the logic of Hindi neo-noir, which is a slightly more complex phenomenon than the urban metropolis/mofussil periphery model that many new realist Hindi films are using. In Hindi neo-noir, the border is porous, allowing the formation of what Bhabha (2004: 28–56) called the third space of enunciation. Thirdness and the porosity of a border give rise to cinematic uncanny related to the off-screen reality. It all can be observed in new Hindi cinema: anxieties over the borders or, more precisely, anxiety over the porous character of borders, return of the repressed, and especially, the identity formation problem.

Identity formation of the neoliberal subject or the formation of the self needs the Other in order for the process to be initiated. In interpreting the Other as a cultural Other, we may say that the Other India is imagined as the imaginary Other for this purpose. Its proximity and the othering of the self that is performed during this process is a cause of anxiety. By Other India, in this context, I mean the interior spaces, both actual and mental, of neoliberal India. Such interior Other space can be the badlands of the periphery, violence in small-town India and it can also be the urban interior—in-between urban spaces outside the new middle class's domain or the mental interior of the middle class itself—a complex lifeworld that can be far more brutal than the estheticized exterior. The latter problem is central in many of Anurag Kashyap's films, as well as in the works of other film-makers working within the neo-noir film form—the complexity of interior and exterior, spatial overlapping and the excavation of the hidden, repressed, *unrepresentable* interior.

Dark cinematic visions, so central to the new Hindi film imaginary, unmask the dualism of the façade of livable present and the horrific, unseen interior. Unseen interior may be interpreted as the social unconscious, and in our case, of India's post-liberalization dream. Neoliberalism does project itself as a perfect regime offering prosperity, freedom and well-being to all embracing it. As many scholars agree, the dark side of neoliberalism is far greater than the projected façade (Brown 2003; Harvey 2007). Bleak cinematic imagination offers a darker vision of post-liberalization, and especially but not exclusively, the urban space of India. Such darkness/dirt and light play is indeed the unmasking of neoliberal utopia by transforming it into a dystopian imaginary. As discussed in the introduction, the social roots of such dark cinematic visions lie in the 1980s and relate to the eclipse of Nehruvian developmentalism, the rise of the Hindu Right and the opening up of the markets. The interior space, a space that is hors-champ, off-screen, must not only be perceived metaphorically. It must be understood also as a chronotope, the increasing presence of which has reached the peak in the early 21st century. Most of the films offer stark spatial juxtapositions of darkness and light. The latter relates to the triumphant global metropolis in the form of high-rises, shopping malls, bright billboards, Western-style restaurants, cozy luxury apartments, convenient metro lines with modern trains as opposed to packed and dilapidated Indian Railways trains, and also flyovers, which are not only a convenience but also a spatial movement above and beyond the often lower-middle-class dwellings and slums, and another tool of othering and spatial segmentation. Such spaces can be juxtaposed to their opposites—lower-class apartments, narrow alleys, etc., but more often the façade of such lightness is stripped off to uncover the *meaning* of such spaces for those who dwell and move in them—not the official, political meaning of greatness, investments of transnational capital, convenience, but the function of such spaces in urban India's everyday life. And how the function of new space transforms the experience of phenomena.

If noir and neo-noir are rooted in the experience of urban life, dirty realism emerged as its spatial opposite—the experience of small-town America and American suburbia. However, similar to noir, dirty realism is also prone to transformations and highly diverse cultural translations. Jameson is critical of dirty realism's reduction to necessarily small town, the spatial periphery of a metropolis, and explores the possibilities of postmodern, urban dirty realism, which he finds in "celebrations of a new reality, a new reality-intensification" of cyberpunk (Jameson 1996: 152). New reality is the effect of speed and its newness lies in the transformed experience and perception of phenomena. Jameson bases his argument on such experiences in a metropolis of a Global North, and in the postcolonial South, this works similarly, but differently at the same time. Jameson's reality intensification can be observed in new Hindi cinema, and supplemented with Mazumdar's view on anti-realism (Mazumdar 2010), as well as with the treatment of such esthetics in a transnational space. Reality intensification also relates to what Paul Virilio described as dromology, and the "aesthetics of disappearance"—the transformed relationship of subject to the phenomena, inability to grasp phenomena due to accelerations caused by the cultures of speed, be it the physical speed as part of technological revolution or televisual speed (Virilio 2009). He also claims that cinema no longer represents, but "presents" the view. His is a very different position from the Bazinian preference for realism (Shaviro 2010: 86–149). Due to the speed, cinema, according to Virilio (2009: 60–5; 2012: 59), becomes more and more of a delirious experience akin to traveling at high speed, where the *reality* of space blurs into incomprehensible and indistinguishable greyness. This will explain some of the problems the critics and spectators find in dirty realist cinema, as I will argue later. Jameson in his work on postmodernism spoke of the unrepresentability of the space of multinational capitalism, and his is a position similar to Virilio's (Jameson 1991: 53–4). While it may seem that new reality in flux, a reality emerging out of either social trauma or massive social restructuring, may be celebrated by new esthetics, the problem is more complex. I agree with Jameson's usage of *misérablisme*—what he calls as an earlier version of dirty realism in French literature (Jameson 1996: 153), but with some reservations. Such an approach may be helpful in understanding less complex films fetishizing the Other and creating a carnivalesque on screen (for example, the films of Vishal Bhardwaj), but misérablisme cannot explain the multiple variations *becoming-subhuman* dirty realist cinema often evokes. In order to understand cinematic dirty realism, we must take a broader look.

Dirty Realism: Some Cinematic Variations

Dark imagination, be it noir or dirty realist, cannot be classified and the esthetic expressions are extremely fluid. Different varieties of "darkness" should concern us here, mostly relating to two major issues: spatial transformations in the urban areas causing the emergence of new esthetic sensibilities and ambiguities of experience, and transformations relating to gender dynamics. Apart from the Euro-American culture, other variants of dirty realism are very important to take into account in order to understand it as a part of globalization's dark esthetics.

Thus, noir is a cinema of modernity's spatial darkness, especially the modernist urban confusion—an effect not dissimilar to Baudelaire's, Simmel's or Benjamin's experience and understanding of the effect of transforming urban experience. Neo-noir may be seen as the "end of modernity" esthetic sensibility trying to negotiate the social and spatial effects of what we may call a "postmodern condition". If social and spatial shifts in the post-War period marked the emergence of noir, then neo-noir is marked by the bleakness of the 1970s—the Vietnam war and the effect it had on the American psyche, the Cold War and the constant threat of nuclear annihilation, and the slow emergence of neoliberalism transforming the social space. Once again, the dark city in various shapes and stripes and the commodified non-places emerge as a dominant chronotope.

Bleakness in terms of style, effects of sociocultural transformations producing unrepresentability and art that does not represent but present in an anti-esthetic way are not confined to film noir, of course. My second point of departure is the concept of dirty realism, which is usually associated with a literary movement that began in the United States in the late 1970s with figures like Raymond Carver, Cormac McCarthy, Jayne Anne Phillips and Charles Bukowski, among others. Some of the definitions of dirty realism may involve the "fascination for blue-collar lives", as well as the rise of consumer culture and postmodernism (Jarvis 2001: 192). The notion of dirty realism is usually used in discussing a specific genre in literature dealing with a dark side of everyday life, of individuals in a state of crisis and often self-destructive individualism. This notion is rarely invoked in cinema research and has never been used in analyzing Indian cinemas. Importantly, dirty realism focuses on the everyday life of the working class, undesirables and strangers. In other words, it focuses on the other side of the American dream in the United States that was rapidly embracing neoliberalism under Ronald Reagan's presidency. It focused on neoliberalism's Other, on the Other who had to take in the negative transformative effect of socio-economic change. We may say that both film noir and dirty realism were esthetic responses to social change during different periods in the 20th century's US history.

Dirty realism, just like film noir, is a very diverse form and many film-makers in different parts of the world appropriate elements of such esthetics. First of all, I would like to mention dirty realism both as a literary and cinematic form in Latin America. Manzoni (2011: 59) in her essay on Cuban dirty realist literature, which emerged in the 1980s, relates the new esthetic form and the creation of "hostile space" as a reaction to cultural transformations in Cuba at the time, and the emergence of "urban" literature dealing with the dark side of life in Havana. She states that this relates to "transformations in language and the creation of new esthetics. Journeys, internal migrations, immigration, exile construct new spaces, often outside the material borders, and on the margins of the canon."[2] She refers to bleak new visions, populated by prisons, illegality, degradation and people dwelling on the margins of society. But, contrary to the American dirty realism, Latin American as well as Indian variants are far more urban-centric. León (2005) speaks of "cinema of marginality", referring to many Latin American films—a new form that began to emerge in the late 1970s and 1980s. He relates the emergence of this new form to the crisis of the 1980s and the emergence of film-makers that wanted to distance themselves from heroes and intellectuals, to interpret the people and their history through a different lens. Such a new form flourished in the 1990s, and "shows violence, processes of exclusion generated by the same social institutions that pretend to fight the disastrous effects of economic modernization" (León 2005: 29). First and foremost, Latin American dirty realist cinema problematizes the life in a big city, the corruption of values, marginality, be it in Rio de Janeiro, in Medellín or in Mexico City.[3] Instead of dealing with grand political and social issues that dominated the new realism, dirty Latin American realism

---

[2] All translations from Spanish are mine.

[3] Good examples of such cinema are Columbian film *Rodrigo D: No Futuro* (*Rodrigo D: No Future*, Víctor Gaviria, 1990), Brazilian films *Cidade de Deus* (*City of God*, Fernando Meirelles and Kátia Lund, 2002), *Carandiru* (Hector Babenco, 2003), Mexican film *Amores Perros* (*Love is a Bitch*, Alejandro Gonzales Iñárritu, 2000), among many others.

instead focuses on micropolitics and everyday life on the street (León 2005: 30). This resonates quite well with the esthetic developments in post-liberalization India. No longer do film-makers try to identify themselves with social cinematic missions of the Indian New Wave of the 1970s and, instead, focus on the dark sides of everyday life, and usually in urban areas. In such a move away from the "grand narratives", there are many similarities between Hindi and Latin American dirty realism, although invocation of noir are quite rare in the Latin American case. This is well illustrated by Anurag Kashyap's battle with the Central Board of Film Certification (CBFC) over his first feature film *Paanch* (*Five*, 2003), which was never released. Among the reasons for objecting to the release of the film, the board stated the lack of "social message" and the negativity of characters (Mazzarella 2013: 111). A move away from social messages and "grand narratives" illustrates the newness of the esthetics of unrepresentability, a distancing from realism. Cinematic dirty realism is often accused of being pointless and India's case is no exception to a general tendency. But lack of the message and being "pointless" indicate inability to grasp the rapidly transforming esthetics, or the disappearance of esthetics—something Virilio (2009) feared. However, lamenting the anti-realism and anti-esthetics would not help much to understand the new phenomenon. As Gilles Deleuze's (1995: 178) often-quoted saying goes, "It's not a question of worrying or of hoping for the best, but of finding new weapons." Or of finding new forms of expression for the rapidly transforming (neoliberal) landscape—something dirty realist film-makers are engaged in.

While the 1980s marked the emergence of neoliberalism as the dominant economic doctrine in the United States and the United Kingdom, in this way making its way into Europe, the late 1980s saw the collapse of the Soviet Union, and the entry of neoliberal capitalism into the formerly communist space. This socio-economic "shock", as Naomi Klein (2007) would call it, caused the emergence of a far more difficult, and perhaps the most devastatingly brutal and claustrophobic cinema, which began in the Soviet Union in the 1980s and became very prominent in the 1990s in Russia and other post-Soviet and post-socialist East European states. Seth Graham (2000: 9) in his analysis of Russian dirty realism, or what is termed as *chernukha*,[4] states that this form "emphasized the darkest, bleakest aspects of human life". He, quoting many Russian film scholars analyzing this form, looks at it as an expression of artistic freedom during the perestroika period in the 1980s, an "over-compensation for decades of official concealment of the negative aspects of social reality" and "anti-aesthetic explosion" of Soviet realism (Graham 2000: 12). Therefore, we can argue that similar to film noir in Hollywood and dirty realism in American literary fiction, the Soviet and later Russian "black wave" was a response to sociopolitical transformation, which released new artistic expressions focusing no longer on melodrama, excessiveness and positive aspects of life, but on their opposites.[5] As Graham (2000: 9) says summarizing the themes of chernukha:

> Typical settings are dirty and/or crowded apartments ... littered court-yards ... urban streets at night, beer bars or liquor stores, police stations or prisons, and hospitals. Characters live either in urban isolation or with other members of truncated ... family. Alcoholism and/or drug addiction is de rigueur, as is the general atmosphere of cruelty....

In short, what is presented is "a nightmare of communal squalor, curses of history, cruel and joyless sex, food line brutality, and the metallic scrape of barracks and prisons" (Graham 2000: 9). Such a "nightmare of everyday life" is far subtler in literary dirty realism, how-ever. Similar elements could be observed in post-Cold War American neo-noir and dirty realism of Quentin Tarantino,[6] and Hindi neo-noir

---

[4] The term can be translated as "blackness".

[5] Good examples of Russian dirty realism include *Hell, or, Dossier on Oneself* (Gennadi Beglov, 1989), *Khrustaliov, Get the Car!* (Aleksey German, 1998) and *Cargo 200* (Aleksey Balabanov, 2007), among others.

[6] *Pulp Fiction* (1994) is often held to be a good example of neo-noir. In my view, the best cases of dirty realism are Tarantino's *Reservoir Dogs* (1992) and *Jackie Brown* (1997). Here Tarantino, in fact, comes closest to the literary American dirty realism. Speaking of dirty realism in the United States, Martin

or Hindi cinematic dirty realism, especially in Anurag Kashyap's films. Most importantly, all the esthetic transformations I discussed are related to rapid social transformations bringing about new forms of expression, sometimes existentialist, but more often nihilistic, pessimistic, reflecting the uncanny of society undergoing such change, but as well as acting as a mode of social criticism. The latter function can be debated, of course, as the line separating social critique and seemingly critical art functioning within the limits set by the system is thin.

Mažeikis goes even further claiming that cinematic dirty realism reflects the ultimate degradation of humanity—something that simple portrayals of poverty, sex, alcoholism or drug usage cannot. For him, "dirt" means reaching the bottom that is so deep that one crosses into a space beyond being human.[7] As a good example of such an esthetic form, he holds Pier Paolo Pasolini's *Salò o le 120 giornate di Sodoma* (*Salò, or 120 days of Sodom*, 1975). He introduces a term "dialectic dirty realism", a goal of which is to

> uncover the road to degradation; not the stairway to heaven but to hell, not into perfection, but into the bottom. Its goal is not to be a representation of horror or to invoke only lust, sadism, or sodomy; what's important is to actualize disappointment, to embody and to consolidate

---

Scorsese's *Taxi Driver* (1976) and, more recently, popular TV series *Breaking Bad* (2008–2013) are good examples of such esthetics. Film noir resurrected in European cinemas and especially TV series over the past decade. The best example may be the so-called Scandinavian noir TV series (like *Forbrydelsen* [*The Killing*, 2007–2012, Denmark], or *Bron/Broen* (*The Bridge*, 2011–2015, Sweden/Denmark), becoming a global phenomenon). I would argue that this cinematic form is also a result of social transformations, and in this case, an attempt to grasp immigration from largely Eastern Europe and the Middle East/ North Africa into, mostly, Sweden and Denmark. Most of the films and TV series try to negotiate the question of the cultural Other, which is a threat to a Scandinavian social order. In this way, Scandinavian noir is a right-wing reaction to the "trauma" of multicultural existence.

[7] Personal conversation with Gintautas Mažeikis in Kaunas, Lithuania, November 2015.

unbelief, rejection, which don't have a direct expression in films, and are not represented, displayed. Heroes are not disappointed with life, but desperately flounder into the bottom.[8] (Mažeikis 2015)

This is a somewhat radical position, but some of Mažeikis's ideas indeed reflect the problems at the heart of Hindi noir or Hindi dirty realist imaginary. I look at the emergence of Hindi noir and dirty realism, their seemingly 'pointless' portrayal of marginal lives as an affective map, following Shaviro (2010) and Jameson (1991) on unrepresentability of the space of multinational capital, as well as Virilio (2009) on the esthetics of disappearance and the disappearance of esthetics. Shaviro calls this mapping the "aesthetic of affective mapping", with reference to Jameson and Deleuze and Guattari (Shaviro 2010: 18). The nihilistic character of new Hindi cinema's noir and dirty realist imaginary is usually marked by the absence of heroes and the nonexistence of anti-heroes. But in this de-individualized void, it is the city that emerges as a silent protagonist imposing itself and shaping the lives of those who dwell in it. Such a mental "masterplan" is populated by self-destructive individuals existing in the dark areas that more often than not are concealed from vision. Concealment is part of neoliberal spatial politics, where only the majestic outside space of capital is constructed, but at the same time, it is part of the dromological politics, where the dark space is blurred by the velocity of mediatized existence.

However, if literary dirty realism in its original form may seem to be a rather clear category, cinematic dirty realism remains a somewhat ambiguous one. Jameson in his discussion on dirty realism quotes Bill Buford, who coined the term in the first place, discussing the new American short story of the late 1970s. Buford says the following about the protagonists of these narratives: "they could just about be from anywhere: drifters in a world cluttered with junk food and the oppressive details of modern consumerism" (as quoted in Jameson 1994: 145). Characters in Hindi neo-noir and dirty realism are also "drifters" in many different ways, like Ruth (Kalki Koechlin) in Anurag

---

[8] Translation from the Lithuanian original is mine.

Kashyap's *That Girl in Yellow Boots* (2010). And when I say "drifter", I do not have a direct understanding of this word. Drifter for me is first and foremost a nomad crossing over the spatial boundaries with ease, thereby producing paranoiac visions and neurotic perceptions.

That Girl in Yellow Boots

Graham (2000: 11) quotes some of the Russian film critics who were skeptical about chernukha's "meaning" and emphasized the meaninglessness of this new form. Similar problems arise looking at Hindi noir, but the problem is not in the "meaning" or lack thereof. This is the phenomena of disappearance or disappearance of phenomena, and inability to relate to the phenomena. This is the case of cinematic "presentability": these films are less cinematic representations, but affective maps, as Shaviro (2010) suggested. And in this sense, Anurag Kashyap is a good example of such a "cartographer". All of his bleak, and sometimes grotesque, films have elements of *darkness and dirt*, if we look at these phenomena as free-flowing esthetic elements that can be assembled and connected in a rhizomatic way: *Paanch* (2003, unreleased), *Black Friday* (2004), *No Smoking* (2007), *Dev D* (2009), *Gulaal* (2009), *That Girl In Yellow Boots* (2010), a two-part *Gangs of Wasseypur* (2012), *Ugly* (2013), a segment in an anthology film *Bombay Talkies* (2013), a very overt homage to film noir *Bombay Velvet* (2015) and *Raman Raghav 2.0* (2016). As he himself admits, he is a huge fan of film noir and noir largely inspired his first film *Paanch*.

Kashyap, in addition to being a director, is also a scriptwriter and a producer, and not only of his own films. He mentors other young film-makers creating similar dark and dirty cinema. He has also acted in some of the films, sometimes playing himself or a role resembling his own biographical details and his childhood or early career experiences. Given his biography, I would say that many of his films contain a lot from his own life as a struggling director (Mazzarella 2003: 110–14). Kashyap himself admits that many of his film scripts come from his own experiences (Khanna 2013). Rahul in *Ugly* in some ways resembles a man trying to make it big in film business. *Udaan* (Vikramaditya

Motwane, 2010), a film co-written and produced by Kashyap, contains autobiographical details from his childhood. A segment directed by him in *Bombay Talkies* about a young man's arrival from a mofussil to Mumbai and his desperation to meet Amitabh Bachchan also reflects fascination with the dream world of cinema as well as his sleeping on the pavement—something Kashyap had to do when he came to Mumbai. He co-produced Michael Winterbottom's *Trishna* (2011) and played himself in the film. In Onir's *I Am* (2010), he played a pedophile (he admits he was sexually abused as a child), a scriptwriter in Zoya Akhtar's *Luck by Chance* (2009), a mafia don in Dhulia's *Shagird* and a corrupt, homicidal police officer in *Akira* (A.R. Murugadoss, 2016).

The film *That Girl in Yellow Boots* presents a more nuanced case of dirty realism and the uncanny city. There is no violence as such in this film, but the lack of it and only a vague sense of dirty off-screen reality is an element making this film a powerful dirty realist mental map. The film is the story of Ruth (Kalki Koechlin), a girl coming from Brighton to Mumbai to look for her father whom she does not even remember. Her mother is English and her Indian father left the family after he sexually abused her older half-sister, who later got pregnant and killed herself. Ruth was too young to remember that and she has to learn this shocking truth by herself in a painful way. The film is shot with a digital camera and the city itself is an important character in the film, and one perhaps may say, one of the authors of the film.

Ruth illegally works as a masseuse (she only has a tourist visa and manages to extend it by bribing relevant officials) and forges friendships with several people, like an elderly gentleman Divakar (Naseeruddin Shah), who is her client and comes both to have a massage and to talk, and sometimes to complain about the hectic urban life. She has a troubled relationship with her drug-addict boyfriend Prashant (Prashant Prakash) and is trying to trace her father. She does not know what he looks like; she only knows his name. She does not earn much working as a masseuse; therefore, for some male clients, she offers what she calls a "handshake" or "happy ending"—a hand job at the end of the massage for Rs 1000. She often wears yellow boots, hence, the title of the film. But the title, especially the phrase "that girl" reveals something else—anonymity, where the only marker of the girl's unique identity is the pair of bright yellow boots only few people wear. At the beginning of the film, she massages a man named Linn. The camera closes in and shows the massage accessories on the table, and next to them, a bottle of Durex Play lubricant. This is the first hint at what Ruth also does besides giving a massage. Linn is her most loyal customer and comes every day to have a "handshake". Later in the film, she manages to establish contact with her father, and he turns out to be no one else but Linn. He knows very well that Ruth is his own daughter, and as he later says, he agreed to have a "handshake" when Ruth first casually offered it because he loved her. He says to Ruth that he sexually abused her half-sister also out of love. This is the ending of the film. She pursues truth, only to uncover a horrific interior beneath the façade.

That Girl in Yellow Boots has some similarities with another film, by Kashyap, dealing with sexual anxiety, mostly male, like *Ugly*, which I shall discuss in the next chapter. Though shocked at first, most of Ruth's clients do accept a "handshake" when offered, and in these scenes, Ruth is very much in control of the man's body, as well as his mind. For unnamed reasons, she is unable to have sexual intercourse, which we perhaps could relate to a repressed trauma in her childhood, her father's sexual abuse of her half-sister. Consciously, she does not remember this, but her inability to have sex raises some questions. In one scene, Ruth refuses to have sex with her boyfriend and instead gives him a hand job. Also, in order to repay a large amount of money that her junkie boyfriend owes to a local mafia boss, she offers to repay in hand jobs. In a scene toward the end of the film, the mafia boss comes to her massage parlor, but when it is time to receive a hand job, he becomes petrified and it is difficult to understand why. He pleads with Ruth to do a hand job without looking at his genitals. A possible explanation might be a loss of control at the hands of a woman, while the actual sexual intercourse might make him dominant. Such male insecurities might be explained by interpreting them vis-à-vis the classic noir's negotiations of sexuality and the white male's fear of diminishing dominance. In a similar way that the transforming social and gender relations in mid-20th-century America were translated into cinematic form, transforming social space in late 20th-century urban India evokes uncertainties, anxieties and the desire for an impossible object—clarity, certainty and serenity.

This film offers deeper insights into the dirty realities of everyday life in a city than many other Kashyap films, and in my view, precisely because of the absence of actual violence. Ruth, in many ways, is a homeless anonymous person in a city, which becomes her temporary home. The digital and often moving camera evokes the feeling of the transitory spaces of a metropolis. Layer by layer, Kashyap peels off the exterior, which consists of "that girl" looking for her father and in process revealing the different kinds of spaces in the city—the massage parlor where men come to satisfy their desires; streets; trains and buses; drug usage.

Titli, B.A. Pass and *Moh Maya Money*

Titli (Kanu Behl, 2014), in all its hopelessness and spatiality, is one such example, containing many important elements discussed earlier. The narrative focuses on a family of car thieves—three brothers, living in a lower-class neighborhood in Delhi with their father. Titli (Shashank Arora) is the youngest one, wishing to escape the claustrophobic existence of life on the margins. The spaces where the film is shot can be divided into three groups: the suffocating dwelling in a lower-class neighborhood; the non-places—a shopping mall and an apartment building construction site on the unnamed outskirts of the city; and a trajectory connecting these distinct spaces—streets, highways, flyovers, cars, buses and metro. The new emplacements of a shopping mall and apartment building are yet to emerge; both are being built and are incomplete. The film in its spatiality does not uncover the façade of the present. It shows the interior whose façade is not yet constructed, something usually blocked from the eyes of onlookers—the interior of a mall and an apartment building under construction.

The film portrays such the hopeless existence of Titli and his brothers. As part of an illegal deal, Titli wants to "purchase" a parking space in an underground parking lot, which would in the future generate income—he would receive the parking fees once the customers actually begin to park their cars. When they are not involved in their official duties, the three brothers steal cars and assault the car owners. At the same time the film also departs from what can be called a classic dirty realism in the sense that Titli wants to get out of such a life, he wants to leave. Whenever Titli is in the frame, his face is both depressed and pensive; he looks at the city, either from a scooter or a bus. At the beginning of the film, Titli visits the shopping mall construction site. When he is leaving on a scooter, he looks back at an emerging skeleton of the mall, and there is something unsettling in his facial expression—as if the skeleton is menacing.

Similar spatial politics and urban claustrophobia is evoked in *B.A. Pass* (Ajay Bahl, 2012). After the death of his parents, Mukesh (Shadab Kamal) lives with his aunt and uncle in a lower-middle-class dwelling in Delhi and passes his time in the cemetery playing chess with a gravedigger Johnny (Dibyendu Bhattacharya), who wants to leave his miserly existence and go to Dubai. He starts a relationship with an older woman Sarika (Shilpa Shukla), who turns out to be a procurer and, in the process, becomes a sex worker. There are just several scenes showing Mukesh's "home"; more often, it is Sarika's luxury bungalow or the crammed spaces in Paharganj where Johnny lives or buses and metro trains. Similar to Titli, Mukesh wants to get out of the kind of life he lives—he tries to make money and has dreams that are, in the end, shattered. The city consumes him and the film ends with his suicide—a leap from the roof of a building in Old Delhi. *B.A. Pass* has an element that *Titli* does not: an almost classical femme fatale, Sarika, who seduces an "innocent" young man and destroys him.

In their own way, they actively participate in the transformations and do try to make use of them while the city crushes them. Titli tries to make money from an abstract space of a mall's parking lot, which does not yet exist, and Mukesh is selling his body. Both Titli and Mukesh are the Others of transnational capital; they are the precariat and what Bauman (2004) has termed as "wasted lives". They are also the Other of the class that is the aspirational one—those who have reaped the fruits of "shining" India. But lives of this segment of society are also truncated and plagued by the constant spatial uncanniness of the city, which is built for them and by them. While *Titli* and *B.A. Pass* depict the shattered lifeworlds of the lower middle class or lower class who live in the shadow of transnational capital and the urban transformation, *Moh Maya Money* (Munish Bhardwaj, 2016) shows the anxious existence of the upper middle class desiring to be "world class"—a desire ultimately leading to tragedy. Aman (Ranvir Shorey) and Divya (Neha Dhupia) are a married couple living in Delhi. She works in television and he is a real estate agent. Aman is very unhappy with their material environment that signifies their belonging to the middle class: they live in a cozy but a rather down-market apartment, and the salary they both are getting does not allow for anything else. But Aman invents a money-making scheme involving real estate speculations, and purchases a plot of land for a house in Delhi. Things never go as planned for him, and he ends up unemployed, indebted and without the plot of land. To pay his debts, he stages his own death. What he does not know is that his beloved wife not only does not share his dreams for "world class" living, but also has an affair with her boss. At the end of this bleak film, after a string of unsuccessful attempts to live a better life, a life forged in the dreamworld of advertisement and neoliberal promises, Aman dies. The uncanny emerges in such dreamed-up and desired luxury spaces and "world class" life in its full force, and the line separating *heimlich* from *unheimlich* disappears.

5

SCREENING MASCULINE ANXIETY
Men, Women and Violence

Raghav and Simmy are a troubled and tragic couple in *Raman Raghav 2.0*. They meet at a nightclub and enter into a "sex only" relationship. In one scene, after having sex, Simmy asks Raghav if he would marry her, to which Raghav—a police officer and a drug addict—reacts violently. He reminds her of their "arrangement" regarding the relationship, which was about sex. He then takes his gun and begins threatening her, moving the gun toward her, but is interrupted when Simmy's phone starts ringing. It is her mother calling. She picks up the phone and starts talking, as if nothing was happening, pushing Raghav and his gun aside and leaving him sitting on the bed astonished with a gun in his hand. Simmy does not fear him. A threatening man with a gun for her is, apparently, a joke, which leaves Raghav at a loss: he does not know what he should do next, how he should act or adapt to a power balance that has suddenly shifted. After finishing her conversation on the phone, Simmy comes back, sits on the bed and nonchalantly asks Raghav what was he trying to say with that gun in his hand. Raghav goes into the bathroom and cries and perhaps the idea of suicide crosses his mind—not living may be a more tempting option than living in a setting where one has to be humiliated by a woman. A woman is his object of desire, as he clearly needs one, but at the same time, a powerful woman is too big a challenge for him to handle. Failing patriarchal authority, masculine anxiety, feeling at a loss in the face of a powerful woman, desire and hatred for women and an all-pervasive feeling of feminine threat—these are always some of the main threads of analysis of film noir. In Hindi neo-noir cinema, this theme is very prominent and *Raman Raghav 2.0* is one of the best examples of what is variously called a masculine protest, a masculine anxiety or wounded masculinity. The film, just as most of the films by Anurag Kashyap, exposes the dirty interior of a contemporary metropolis, an interior hidden by an often mundane or beautiful façade. Also, he exposes a problem that was always central to noir imaginary—masculine anxiety in a fast-changing urban space. This adds another, and a very important, layer to the problems explored in previous chapters. Next to the emerging uncanny and urban dislocation, next to the transforming middle class identities there is a transforming gender disequilibrium, as well as the attempts to re-assert the masculinity in a 21st-century Indian metropolis. What happened to masculinity that it would need reassertion? What kind of trauma befell men that their masculinity is under threat? Which type of masculinity? Literature exploring masculine anxieties or their representations in the modern era is rich and diverse, ranging from psychoanalysis to sociology and from philosophy to film theory (Parsons 1954; Adler 1956; Carrigan, Connell and Lee 1985; Connell 2005; Lehman 2007). In this chapter, I shall reflect on the rise of masculine anxiety in post-liberalization India and its representation in new Hindi cinema vis-à-vis the representation of a strong woman, and at times, what has been termed, in film noir, as a femme fatale, a woman posing an existential threat to the hero. The case of global neo-noir is far more complex in this regard, as the image of a woman as threatening a masculine self is not always clear-cut. On the contrary, quite often, films portray strong women or even women as the heroines of noir thrillers. New Hindi cinema, in this regard follows in the footsteps of global noir, although the dark films of the 1990s are keeping a woman "safely" at the distance, for example, the films of Ram Gopal Varma, whom I discussed earlier and to whom I shall return in this chapter. This chapter, by analyzing some of the key films of new Hindi cinema, argues that without understanding the shifts in masculine identity, it is not possible to understand the dark nature of new Hindi cinema fully; gender is one of the key aspects of film noir. The relationship between men and women, as well as masculine violence—both toward the woman and self-destructive toward oneself—has to be seen as a reaction to the transforming social, cultural and political landscape. Masculine anxiety or masculine protest is a defensive reaction against the loss of authority, and more generally, a reaction to the fast-changing circumstances, a reaction of dromological existence and the liquidity of what once was solid. The effect of all this is uncertainty, which, as I discussed in previous chapters, results in different types of fear. Excessive masculinity or male violence attempts to reassert authority and hypermasculine imaginary—all of these are means to combat fear. In this chapter, I shall discuss a reaction to shifting notions of femininity and gender balance, something that was a direct effect of liberalization. Slavoj Žižek (2007: 178), in a different but related context, asks: "What change had to befall the symbolic order, so that woman finds herself occupying the place of the traumatic Thing?". Anxious masculinity places a woman at the center of the discourse, and this time, a woman, always already objectified, becomes a site of gendered negotiations of existence in the India transformed by neoliberal ideology. In trying to answer these questions in an Indian context by looking through cinema, first we must frame the problem by looking at the roots of masculine protest in cinema, and by analyzing the moment of change in India—the economic liberalization.

The "New Indian Woman" Discourse

I would like to briefly reflect on the changing concept of femininity in India in the late 1980s and early 1990s. The change was an effect of the liberalization process, in which, among other issues, a "new" and liberalized nation needed a new type of woman, an emancipated but also a desiring consumer (Rajagopal 2001). Thus, the new woman had to be, as it has been throughout the 20th century, an amalgam of tradition and modernity. As Purnima Mankekar (1999b: 106) notes, "the 'uplift' of women became a crucial component of state's agenda to construct a modern national culture". Newness of this type had to be forged as "India and Indian women have emerged out of decades of state control and finally have the opportunity to express themselves" (Oza 2006: 25). Importantly, the "New Liberal Indian Woman" who entered the popular imagination as an icon of Indian neoliberal modernity was primarily being constructed in the spheres of advertisement, television serials, newspapers, magazines and talk shows (Mankekar 1999b; Oza 2006). Liberated, emancipated, just like "New India", the new woman was ready to face the global challenges and the 21st century. Here lies the fundamental problem: just like in the nationalist discourse in colonial India, the woman and the nation were mirroring one another, and nationalist, deeply patriarchal mentality does not necessarily go hand-in-hand with the kind of liberation neoliberalism and free market economy usually offers. As Rupal Oza (2006: 27) notes, "the discourse of the new woman implies that the liberalization of the economy opens up spaces and possibilities for Indian women to express themselves and satisfy their aspirations in ways not previously possible in a closed economy".

Liberalization of economy meant more job opportunities for women in the corporate sector, where they had to compete with men, and ultimately be in the public domain. It also meant availability of a vast array of consumer goods, cosmetics, clothing and appliances directed at women consumers. Satellite television and the uncensored and uncontrolled broadcasting of Western media had a significant impact on the shifting understanding of the world and shifting identities, and among them, gender identities. The construction of a "global desi" in the 1990s was also an important part of negotiating shifting gender roles in a transformed sociocultural space. If Shah Rukh Khan's heroes became the prototypes of a new man for a newly "freed" nation, negotiating the construction of a new woman was ambivalent, as the woman, just as in the imagination of colonial modernity, had to be modern yet traditional; independent, professional, but also remaining a repository of tradition. Here, the films like *Dilwale Dulhania Le Jayenge* and *Kabhi Khushi Kabhie Gham* are interesting, especially the hero's love interests—Simran in the former and Anjali in the latter, both played by Kajol. They were women bowing down in front of the patriarchal authority, but simultaneously independent and liberated. Such women were able to be love interests of a "new Indian man": women not entirely Westernized, even if they were part of the diaspora. Both Simran and Anjali, although having transgressive elements like love marriage, were functioning entirely in a patriarchal universe, accepting the patriarchy as part of culture and tradition; questioning it, but to a certain limit. Such was the ideal conservative vision of a "New Liberal Indian Woman", and such was her construction in Bollywood, but the realities were different. Gender emancipation that was triggered by liberalization was never conceived as "partial", and feminism on the intellectual plane went strongly against the values of patriarchal nationalism. Also, liberalization means sexual liberalization as well, which goes against the patriarchal core. Such emancipation can and often does result in moral panic, which, in our case, has to be somehow channeled out, negotiated. Representation of a woman in new Hindi cinema as strong, independent, suffering from patriarchal authority and not bowing down is the result of cinematic negotiations since the early 1990s. In such a scenario, the hegemonic or pre-neoliberal masculinity finds itself under siege, and the anxiety I shall talk about is primarily the anxiety of hegemonic masculinity. As Lynne Segal (2007) claims in her research on masculinities, shifting economic and cultural patterns, among other issues, significantly contribute to male insecurity vis-à-vis women. One possible outcome of this is the rise of hypermasculinity, or, in other words, of masculine protest as a means to mask weakness.

The relationship between social reality and cinema in post-liberalization India is uncannily similar to the relationship of the classic noir and the social reality of the mid-20th-century America. The stronger presence of a woman in the public space and stronger assertions of individuality and sexuality "traumatize" the patriarchal order, and the trauma finds a cinematic expression through what has become the global noir. Since its rise in the 1990s, this form, which in its own right is a cinema of globalization, has responded to various traumatizing manifestations of neoliberal globalization in the world: urbanization and poverty in Latin America, the uncanny immigrant figure in Europe, urbanization in South East Asia, the trauma of the collapse of USSR in Eastern Europe, etc. In India, neo-noir comes back closer to its roots by making sexuality, and especially masculine protest, one of the central chronotopes.

Wounded Masculinities and Post-Feminist Imaginaries

Questions of violence, of being a wounded man and of middle-class masculine homelessness, literal and metaphorical, can be read in *Badlapur* (Sriram Raghavan, 2015), although in a very different sense; masculine anxiety is absent in this film. During the bank robbery, Liak (Nawazuddin Siddiqui) and Harman (Vinay Pathak) kill a woman named Misha (Yami Gautam) and her son Robin. Raghav (Varun Dhawan), a husband and a father working in the advertisement sector, is devastated. The police catch Liak, who is sentenced to 15 years in prison—located in the town of Badlapur—for the murder, but fails to capture Harman, whose identity remains unknown to them. Raghav moves from Pune to Badlapur and, for 15 years, waits for a moment to have his revenge. He lives in a dingy and half-empty apartment and works as a manager at a factory. Although he lives in the apartment for years, it has no resemblance of home space. It is solitary and dejected, a transitory space where he only stays temporarily, paying no attention to bodily or material comforts, and waits. It is a kind of purgatory, where Raghav waits for a moment to avenge the murder, and in the process of revenge seeking, he becomes the man he pursues and wants to murder. With revenge being his aim, he completely disregards others and brings pain and violence to all those crossing his path, most importantly, to women. Women are instruments Raghav uses to achieve his goals. There are three women he is using: Jhimli (Huma Qureshi)—a good-hearted prostitute and Liak's girlfriend; Kanchan (Radhika Apte)—Harman's wife, who knows nothing of her husband's past; Shobha (Divya Dutta)—a liberal fighter for prisoners' rights.

While on the run, Liak gets arrested and Harman runs away with the money. Years later, he is shown as a successful restaurant owner, married to Kanchan, whom Raghav uses to get close to their family.

In the end, he kills both of them in a fit of anger. As Liak has cancer, Shobha is fighting for his release, and Raghav seduces her and sleeps with her. All women here are Raghav's symptoms and he uses them by utilizing the dormant hypermasculine self. Sex, sexual threats and rape are the elements Raghav uses against all three women and he does not remonstrate any kind of remorse for his actions. In the end, he manages to get away with all the murders he commits, but there is little satisfaction in his eyes. From a middle-class everyman, he transforms into a murderer—someone and something he was fighting against. *Badlapur* focuses on what happens when the inner, dormant self is resurrected. A self that dwells in the ruins of destruction and destitution. Some of the New Hindi cinema films I shall discuss, by focusing on troubled, violent, traumatized and traumatizing male characters, produce a critical perspective on male violence and masculine protest, and demonstrate one tendency related to this phenomenon—that such a protest, the roots of which lie in social and cultural, as well as economic transformations, leads to the destruction of self and Other, where the Other is always a woman, threatening, alluring, but always already needed to be, and refusing to be submissive to the dreams and desires of hegemonic masculinity.

According to Alfred Adler, who coined the term "masculine protest", the emphasis on masculinity and excessive, violent manifestations of masculinity occur due to anxiety, which is the result of weakness:

> The structure of the neuroses (neurasthenia, hysteria, phobia, paranoia, and especially compulsion neurosis) shows the often ramified feminine traits carefully hidden by hypertrophied masculine wishes and efforts. This is the masculine protest.... The masculine protest intensifies the desires of the child, who then seeks to surpass the father in every respect and comes into conflict with him. (Adler 1956: 48)

Adler, in opposition to Freud, thought masculine protest to be central to neurosis. Neurosis, as I have already demonstrated, can be a useful concept in understanding a particular type of imagination. It is important to note that for Adler, the terms "masculinity" and "femininity" are synonyms for strength and weakness, and should not be read directly. Also, masculine protest is never reserved to men only; in Adlerian understanding, women who demonstrate strength also demonstrate masculine protest, a protest vis-à-vis the existing power relations. Sigmund Freud (2012), who used Adler's concept in theorizing narcissism, calls the masculine protest a "castration complex" and sees it as narcissistic in nature. Such psychoanalytical claims that such type of masculinity is a manifestation of neurosis are shared by sociology as well. In his study of aggression, Talcott Parsons (1954: 300) claims that such neurosis appears when security, mostly in relationships and in childhood, is under threat, leading to development of fear. Parsons also relates the emergence of this problem due to the inability to do something one is expected to—a feeling of inadequacy. Looking at the problem faced by males in late 20th-century India, what is a man expected to do and cannot do? There may be many answers to this question. Inability to accept gender equality may be one. Inability to be a "new liberal Indian man", given the baggage of patriarchy one has to bear. Tensions arising from tough competition in the job market and difficulties in successfully living the dream of "global India"? Tensions due to loss of power and authority? There may be many similar answers, and different combinations of problems and circumstances leading to the development of a neurotic condition of masculine anxiety and an imaginary wound a man bears. But one thing must be clear and has to be at the start of every inquiry into this issue: the shifting social, economic and cultural landscape and the rise of the "new liberal Indian woman" triggered the so-called masculine protest in India beginning in the 1990s.

Variations of a cynical male character—unattached, unkempt, drinking, at times psychotic and misogynist—populates noir and dirty realist imagination globally. Interpretation of noir as male anxiety in a post-War United States and its various transformations informing diverse cinematic and literary imaginations has become canonical (Krutnik 1991; Sobchack 1998; Abbott 2002; Lindop 2015). R.W. Connell (2005: 18), drawing upon Adler and commenting on the Frankfurt school's study on authoritarian personality and the rise of fascism in Germany, states that "the 'authoritarian' type was a masculinity particularly involved in the maintenance of patriarchy: marked by hatred for homosexuals and contempt for women, as well as a more general conformity to authority from above, and aggression towards the less powerful".

Patrice Petro (1989: xxi), though without any reference to noir, in a critique of Weimar cinema's interpretation as an expression of male anxiety, states that such films are usually understood

> as a genre that displaces male anxieties about class identity onto anxieties about women and sexual identity. The male figure's search for sexual excitement, which ends in defeat and regression thus sets up an allegory about male subjectivity that stresses both psychic and social defeat: impotent, passive apparently and object of pity, the male subject in Weimar fails to achieve the kind of mastery necessary for the legitimate functioning of the political, economic, and social order.

These observations try to contextualize the rise of film noir in the United States in the 1940s as a legacy of Weimar cinema and the sociocultural climate of Germany in the 1930s, from where many of the classical noir directors emigrated. But if we look at the context of India in the 1980s and 1990s, we can see striking similarities. Spatial fear and uncertainty brought about by cultural transformations in India started to disrupt the entrenched patriarchal order. As I mentioned in the "Introduction", the 1980s were marked by the rise of the Hindu Right, which was and is masculinist, misogynist and violent. Attempts to imagine a patriarchal family and a submissive son, who is a "global desi" but firmly rooted into what some of the films claim to be tradition, were dominant in the mainstream Bollywood in the 1990s to early 2000s—again, films by Aditya Chopra and Karan Johar being good examples. The space toward which India opened up due to liberalization, the West, was imagined by the "global desis" as a "site of rampant sexuality and promiscuity" (Mankekar 1999a: 736). The gender dynamics in such outside spaces were very much following the pre-globalization pattern. However, both mainstream Bollywood and emerging alternative imaginaries were yet to produce visions filled with anxiety. Dominant popular imagination was still euphoric, still invariably filled with dreams of a bright future in the world. Simultaneously, the 1990s were marked by communal tensions, and the post-Ayodhya period was also marked by films addressing the rise of the Hindu Right and the Hindu–Muslim tensions. Hindi cinema was slow in giving way to paranoiac imagination with openly violent and dislocated men—dislocated in terms of their social position, economic position or both. But in the 2000s, transformations become obvious and embodied. The submissive son who rebels against his father but, in the end, accepts his subordinate position, without the Oedipal complex resolved, in order to live in harmony and happiness[1] gives way to a fallen, disowned and homeless son who is on the path of self-destruction. The type of masculinity that can be observed in India today and a type of masculine imagination that is depicted by cinema signify an unresolved Oedipal complex, attempting to free oneself from the Father, but unable to continue living. Such males are castrated by the transformed social circumstances and are unable to resolve their masculine position after a social dislocation.

Approaching the problem from the cinematic point of view, we must emphasize that the global noir as a film form is generally male-centric, just as the original noir was, where a woman, posing a threat to the male protagonist, or femme fatale, was often a "symptom of a man", to paraphrase Lacan (cited in Žižek 2007: 176–7). Žižek claims that "'woman is a symptom of a man' means that *man himself exists only through woman qua his symptom*" (Žižek 2007: 177). Such a symptom manifests itself as a peculiar warning to masculinity and men. Femme fatale is a metaphor for an independent woman, a woman that in "real life" emerged due to economic pressures, when due to America's participation in World War II, there were not enough men as a workforce and the women had to step outside their prescribed gender roles and

---

[1] The father's approval for marriage as a socially transgressive act in *Dilwale Dulhania Le Jayenge* or *Kabhi Khushi Kabhie Gham* illustrates this problem very well. Films by Sooraj R. Barjatya, who allegedly had a strong influence on Karan Johar's world view, like *Hum Aapke Hain Kaun..!* (1994), *Hum Saath-Saath Hain* (1999) and *Vivah* (2006), also evoke desperate panic of portraying "unchanging values" of patriarchal and necessarily Hindu social order.

assume different ones. Of course, they were expected to go back to their "original" position after the war, once the men returned. Many did, but that only contributed to the rising tensions and male insecurity. An independent working woman was a threat to the patriarchal system. A femme fatale, an excessive representation of such a woman, acted as a warning of what would happen if women would assume a position of power or actually be like the femme fatale: they would castrate the man. As we shall see later, this is the source of what Alfred Adler termed a masculine protest. Thus, the femme fatale in classic film noir is usually a cunning woman pretending to care for the male protagonist, to be attracted to him, to be in need of his help, who in one way or the other seduces a man causing his downfall. This can be seen as an expression of male castration anxiety. A good example of the femme fatale in Bollywood and pre-Bollywood Hindi cinema is a vamp. The vamp, as many authors have suggested, acted as an object of male desire and was outside the social realm; she was a woman squarely for enjoyment. In the 1990s, however, the heroine herself started performing the item numbers, and the figure of a homely woman blended with the vamp. The vamp can be seen entirely as a voyeuristic male fantasy, as a way to deal with the male castration anxiety (Mulvey 1989: 21). In new Hindi cinema, the item number disappears almost entirely. The period of the vamp was a period of stable patriarchal relations. The breakdown of the vamp and her incorporation into reality can be seen as a rising fear regarding the shifting role of women in society. Intensification of such a shift became increasingly prominent after the liberalization. The vamp can be seen as a deadly woman, and the merging of the heroine and the vamp—as a recognizable woman becoming deadly. Similar mutations in the symbolic order can be observed in many, if not most, neo-noir films of new Hindi cinema.

According to Adler (1956: 47), "all neurotics have a childhood behind them in which they were moved by doubt regarding the achievement of full masculinity. The renunciation of masculinity, however, appears to the child as synonymous with femininity". In the anthology film *Bombay Talkies* (2013), in the segment directed by Zoya Akhtar, a young boy Vicky dreams of being Katrina Kaif, dresses up as a woman and dances to the popular Bollywood song "Sheila ki Jawaani". His father is outraged. As per his father's desire, he plays football, although he hates it, and feels useless doing it. He would rather play the piano. Similarly, in *Udaan* (Vikramaditya Motwane, 2010), Rohan, a teenage boy, returns from a boarding school to his father's home in Jamshedpur and lives in the shadow of extreme patriarchal authority. He dreams of going to Mumbai and working at a friend's father's restaurant. A neurotic man having a difficult childhood in terms of rivalry with the father, unresolved Oedipal complex—this can be used to explain the rise of masculine protest in present-day India. New Hindi cinema offers a way to understand this complex issue.

Classic noir responded to particular social settings, and the masculine anxiety in the films of the mid-20th century can be thus contextualized. Why does neo-noir, emerging in the 1970s and becoming a global noir in the 1990s, still retain, to a very large extent, strongly masculinist elements? Samantha Lindop (2015: 11) relates this to post-feminism. According to her, "postfeminism is a patriarchally grounded, media inspired concept that promotes the individualistic, consumer driven rhetoric of neoliberalism, while shying away from political engagement, instead functioning as a closed loop rhetoric that begins and ends with the media, popular culture, and advertising".

She further claims that the central themes of post-feminism are played out in neo-noir, and one should explore it "in the context of the socio-political climate of neoliberalism" (Lindop 2015: 14). Neoliberalism, as already mentioned, works through the valorization of the individual as an entrepreneur, as calculating, self-regulating and autonomous. The forging and internalization of a new subjectivity during the global rise of neoliberalism in the 1990s after the collapse of the Soviet Union had widespread global impact, and today such "values" are dominant and rarely questioned. According to Lindop (2015: 14–15), they correspond to the character traits of the femme fatale. Post-feminism, thus, can be seen as a response to feminism, but at the same time, as an integral element in the logic of neoliberalism. Noir-ish qualities of the femme fatale have become *the* qualities for all disregarding the gender. But precisely here, the tensions arise. "Fit-for-all" neoliberal values are an ideal model. In reality, a woman is still expected to be feminine and conform to the patriarchal reading of values—getting married, having children, but at the same time having a career. Global noir, which Lindop understands as a post-feminist cinema, emerges in the 1990s out of these tensions and neoliberal values, pushing the individualistic and success-driven subjectivity as an ideal, once again unmasks the gender-based tensions and masculine anxieties that perhaps were less visible in the decades since the second wave of feminism. However, with the rise of third-wave feminism in the 1990s, global noir has also started gaining prominence as a global phenomenon. For this reason, post-feminism as a backlash against the third-wave feminism is an important social context for the rise of global noir. India's case is different, as the tensions caused by the neoliberal reforms were much stronger than in Europe or the United States, whose cinemas are usually analyzed in this context. And because of this, the masculine anxiety in new Hindi cinema neo-noir comes very close to the paranoiac imagination of classic noir.

To use Žižek's (2007: 174) analysis of film noir, we may be able to say that a woman in such imagination is always off-field (hors-champs). The second important point is that we can view a woman as the Other, as the narrative is always told from the perspective of the male protagonist. As Naremore (2008: 26) explains, even the French critics, who were fascinated with American noir in the 1950s and coined the term itself, were "sometimes treating film noir as it were an existential allegory of the white male condition". In France, film noir was interpreted as an existential cinematic form, having an existential anti-hero at the center. Though Naremore somewhat dismisses the treatment of noir as an "allegory of white male's condition", I would be far more reserved when it comes to new Hindi cinema. Transformed sexuality and gender relations are very much at the center, although often silenced in many new Hindi cinema noir and dirty realist films. Among other important issues, new Hindi cinema noir may also be interpreted, with certain limitations, as the existential allegory of the Indian male's condition in neoliberal India.

In films I discuss in this part, the troubled male characters act in spaces marked by transience, oppression, squalor and ephemerality.

Dev in *Dev D* leaves his parent's house to live a marginal, alcohol-infused existence at a cheap hotel in Delhi. Raghav in *Raman Raghav 2.0*, similarly, lives away from his estranged family with his girlfriend, with whom he shares a "sex only" relationship. Raman in the same film does not seem to have a home at all and, in many ways, can be seen as an invader and disruptor of other homes. These are but some examples. Spatial dislocation as much as a social one is a distinctive feature of neo-noir and dirty realist cinema in general.

Troubled masculinity is being represented in its many shades, and not only in neo-noir cinema—from a confused male trying to assert his failing patriarchal status (Dev in *Dev D*, Vijay in *Queen*), to violent, psychotic, misogynist men (*Raman Raghav 2.0*), to the destruction and castration of an oppressive man by a female (*Ek Hasina Thi*, *NH10*, among others). A thread connecting all these films and forming a pattern or a chronotope is the negotiation of gender relations and an emergence of a strong feminine figure. The dominant academic narrative in film noir studies claims that a strong female or a femme fatale functions as a threat to the patriarchal order, posing an almost existential threat to the male protagonist. Such a psychoanalytical reading of gender relationships in film noir has its benefits, but the muddy waters of neo-noir are more complex and far more resistant to blunt categorization. Should we understand these films as emancipatory tales countering the hegemony? Are they the expressions of the castration fear, and silent warnings to the patriarchic order? Is that the reason why the woman, in the words of Žižek (2007: 178), finds herself occupying the place of a traumatic Thing?

Kaun?

Cinematic manifestation of such thingification of a woman and her transformation into a male-hating figure can be seen in Ram Gopal Varma's *Kaun?* (1999), written by Anurag Kashyap—a film anticipating new Hindi cinema. The film has three characters—two men and a woman. On a stormy day in Mumbai, a woman (Urmila Matondkar), who remains unnamed in the film, is alone at home, in a large house.

In the first scene, she speaks to her mother and, in a girlish voice, tells her how frightened she is to be home alone. A large part of the film deals with a lonely woman's fear of an intruder: fear of the Other disrupting the safe and homely space. Two men, who come to the house uninvited, disrupt what was, apparently, supposed to be an ordinary day. Sameer (Manoj Bajpayee), a fast-talking office worker looking for Mr Malhotra's house, knocks on the door and manages to get himself admitted inside the house due to the heavy rain and storm. The woman feels extremely threatened and suspects that the man wants to harm her. Later, another man arrives, introducing himself as Qureishi (Sushant Singh) and posing as a police officer but, in fact, being a burglar. When it seems that all this is too much to handle for the woman, in one of the rooms of the house, the men discover the body of the house owner, Mr Malhotra, wrapped in a carpet. It is the woman who killed Mr. Malhotra. We do not know if she was an intruder or if she actually lived in the house. She appears to be a mentally disturbed killer and murders the two men. The film ends just as it begins—with the woman calling her imaginary mother and telling her in a girlish voice how frightened she is. The film, which begins as a standard story of a damsel in distress, ends by reversing the *supposed* gender balance. Men, who never felt any potential threat from a seemingly fragile woman and, on the contrary, felt only superiority dictated by their gender, now must fear for their lives. The film is a thriller and barely demonstrates protest masculinity tendencies, but is very subtle in demonstrating how easily the power balance can shift. Sameer does not believe Qureishi is a police officer and sides with the woman in her mistrust. Both men fight, barely paying attention to the woman as a potential threat. As it is expected, the woman in front of them is fragile and scared at the end of the movie; however, she "castrates" both men. The film was released in 1999, almost a decade after the liberalization and new Hindi cinema sensibilities were yet to emerge, signifying broader shifts in imagination. Perhaps that's why the woman is portrayed as mentally ill, and this fact, the fact of irrationality and madness, plays down the fact of feminine strength. The mad woman cannot be regarded as an indicator of a broader change, only as an isolated case of abnormality. This film, to an extent, can be called a "feminine threat" film, although the notion of revenge in this case is problematic. In such films, a woman destroys a man who, in one way or the other, harmed her or her loved ones in the past. In *Kaun?*, the men get punished for being men. They get punished because they never suspect a woman can be dangerous and such is the price they must pay for being naïve.

Ek Hasina Thi

If *Kaun?* cannot be considered as part of a larger tendency in dark cinema, and as a 1990s film that is only anticipating new Hindi cinema, *Ek Hasina Thi*[2] (Sriram Raghavan, 2004) is one of the finest examples of feminine threat and revenge in new Hindi cinema and an extension of themes explored in the former film. Sarika (Urmila Matondkar) is a single woman, working at a travel agency and living alone in Mumbai. The first-half of the film is filled with paranoia and an unnameable threat that Sarika is experiencing, but it is never clear how real the threat is and what are the origins of Sarika's "neurosis". She constantly feels the uncanny presence; she also feels an unnameable threat in her apartment, posed by a neighbor, who is possibly after her. The film presents the classical problem of not feeling at home in one's home. The home here is as unhomely as the street at night, where Sarika is, one day, assaulted by drunk men and is saved by an enigmatic business executive Karan (Saif Ali Khan). Karan in many ways is *homme fatal*—charming, good-looking, courageous, but at the same time, secretive, cunning and violent. Homme fatal, as Lindop (2015: 125–6) explains, is present in female investigative thrillers, where a woman investigator is pursuing a male criminal, who can be violent, cunning, seductive and obsessive. Initially, the film demonstrates the patriarchal gender equation, where a woman is in need of protection and a hero appears to offer her just that. She becomes dependent on Karan and falls madly in love with him. Sarika knows very little of her newly found boyfriend. He travels a lot; he says that his father is in the United States and his

---

2 *Ek Hasina Thi* was produced by Ram Gopal Varma.

mother in Europe, and that they are divorced. When Karan drives away the drunk men who assault Sarika, he breaks one man's hand, although there is no apparent reason for that. At first, Sarika does not trust him but her mistrust crosses a logical limit. When Karan comes to her apartment for the first time, she asks him what he would like with his tea; he says he wants to kiss her. She pushes him away. This scene suggests that Sarika may have had a traumatic past, but we as spectators never learn about it. The film can be divided into two distinct parts. In the first one, Sarika is a naïve victim of a cunning gangster who poses as a charming businessman. She then goes to prison as she was suspected of aiding a gangster, and she then realizes that Karan was using her. The second part of the film focuses on her violent revenge. It is Karan who becomes a hunted victim. The film overall is a bleak vision of present-day urban India. Alienation, the unnameable threat the city evokes in its dwellers, dark spaces and cunning characters populate the map of *Ek Hasina Thi*. It is interesting that in the beginning, it is not clear whether the threats and the presence of the uncanny are real or imagined. At the same time, the film is shot from the perspective of Sarika, and for her, such a presence is very much part of her existence. The first scene of the film acts as a preview into the dark tale we are about to witness. It shows a dark space and a steel plate on the stone floor. The camera shows a rat on the plate, eating leftovers. It then moves on, showing a woman sitting on the floor of what is a dimly lit prison cell, staring into the camera. All this while, a disturbing, haunting music is playing. The first-half of the film manages to create the uncanny atmosphere and confuse the viewer. In the end, Sarika, who is seduced, used and then framed for crimes she never committed, has her revenge and kills Karan. Such feminine threat and revenge films, inside and outside noir, though they have existed before (for example, Prakash Jha's *Mrityudand* (1997)), have proliferated, especially after the Delhi rape in December 2012—a tragedy that caused massive public rage. Many films were released that engage with female emancipation in its many forms—critique of patriarchy and gender violence—or simply have a strong female protagonist who undermines the patriarchal order: *Kahaani* (Sujoy Ghosh, 2012), *Mardaani* (Pradeep Sarkar, 2014), *Gulaab Gang* (Soumik Sen,

2014), *Mary Kom* (Omung Kumar, 2014), *Saala Khadoos* (Sudha Kongara, 2016), *Pink* (Aniruddha Roy Chowdhury, 2016), *Akira* (A.R. Murugadoss, 2016), *Kahaani 2* (Sujoy Ghosh, 2016), *Lipstick Under My Burkha* (Alankrita Shrivastava, 2016), *Mom* (Ravi Udyawar, 2017), among others.

Mom and *Kahaani*

Alfred Adler (1956), as I mentioned before, claims that the phenomenon of masculine protest is not limited to men: it is also a female rebellion against the male hegemony and hegemonic masculinity. At the same time, we must keep in mind that there was nothing "progressive" about film noir and its innovative femme fatale figure. Such a woman was a symptom and a peculiar warning to masculinity—a Thing onto which the trauma was projected. Given the nature of patriarchy to regroup and project a reactionary idea disguised as, in the present case, a "feminist" film, how and where do we locate the emergence of female-centric films, especially those showcasing woman's empowerment as male's disempowerment? Not all of them can be seen as postfeminist, and in this section, I would like to draw upon several of them.

Mom is a clear response to gang rapes, especially in Delhi, reports of which have been soaring over the past few years. Set in Delhi, which on many occasions has been labeled as the rape capital of India, the film focuses on the revenge that follows a gang rape and attempted murder. Arya (Sajal Ali) is a teenage girl, who sets out to attend a party at a nightclub. After leaving the nightclub to go home, she is kidnapped by a group of men, raped and left to die. After this, the film focuses on Arya's stepmother Devki (Sridevi), a high-school teacher, and her attempts to get justice for the crime against her stepdaughter after the court acquits the rapists. Devki, with the help of a private detective D.K. (Nawazuddin Siddiqui), gets one man mutilated, another poisoned, and is forced into a game of cat and mouse with detective Matthew Francis (Akshaye Khanna), who is investigating both the rape and the attacks against the acquitted rapists. In terms of its style, *Mom* is a neo-noir thriller. Interestingly, the first man has his genitals cut off by a group of hijras, Devki's former students. He dies after slipping and hitting his head in the bathroom after realizing that he has been mutilated. *Mom*, essentially, as many other similar films, reverses the hierarchy of violence. If at the beginning of the film, a woman is threatened by a man and experiences fear, assault and insecurity, in the second-half of the film, it is a man who runs for his life and is threatened by a middle-aged, middle-class woman, a mother and a teacher, someone who could be least suspected of acts of violence. Such a reversal makes this and similar films problematic, as it justifies not just any type of violence or violent revenge, but gender-based violence. There were similar films over the past years, like *Gulaab Gang* and *NH10* among others. I have discussed the latter, but from a very different angle. In the second-half of *NH10*, Meera unleashes violent revenge on her husband's killers, killing all of them, and some of them very brutally. While initially, she is threatened, as I argued, by the Other in a more abstract sense, later, she is threatened by violent men. In order to counter the violence, she becomes a violent and avenging woman, just like Devki. Such reversals add little to the discourse on gender equality and gender-based violence in India. One has to keep in mind that rape is, essentially, an exercise of power. It is possible to relate rape to masculine anxiety and see it as a result of this anxiety and as a means to reassert masculinity and control over the female body. Revenge, mutilation and murder of a man are bodily acts as well. In *Mom*, femininity responds to violent masculinity by a bodily act; a woman, in the end, possesses the body of a man, and does to the male body what is most often done to a female one.

Bodily matters are also crucial in *Kahaani*. Vidya Bagchi (Vidya Balan), a pregnant woman based in London, arrives in Kolkata to look for her missing husband. In this film, her pregnancy makes her seem helpless and harmless, but it is only an illusion—a deliberate and effective one. As a pregnant woman in distress, Vidya commands respect and affection from virtually everyone, and till the very last scenes of the film, the narrative does not offer anything striking in terms of gender. Vidya is a woman, men are assisting her and she uses this assistance to the fullest. However, during the fight scene with a terrorist responsible for her husband's death, he kicks her in the belly and, to his shock (and to our amazement), realizes that the belly is fake. Vidya is not pregnant at all, only pretends to be. Within seconds the power balance in the film is reversed. Vidya is a vengeful woman searching for her husband's killer and she kills the terrorist, who is too shocked to do anything at all. His manly demeanor vanishes instantly and he becomes a man under threat. While it would not be easy in the analysis of this film to tease out any comments regarding the masculine anxiety, one issue is clear: the film manipulates the viewers (something *Mom* or *Ek Hasina Thi* do not do), making full use of the dominant gender preconceptions—a pregnant, fragile-looking woman cannot be a threat to anyone. But in both cases, a man is caught unprepared and must face a woman's anger. Such shades of masculinity—from artificial strength and outright fear—are explored by Anurag Kashyap, one of the most important directors in new Hindi cinema, in representing a critical position toward the masculine anxiety.

Anurag Kashyap's Anxious Men: From Self-Destruction to Violence

Kashyap is an experimenting film-maker drawing his influence from a vast array of cinematic traditions, and by doing so, he invents a new film form. His heroes are especially conservative regarding sexuality and gender relations. They fear women. They adore them. Kashyap's women are strong, but always off-field, subjected to male anxieties. Always sexual objects. The only film having a female protagonist is *That Girl in Yellow Boots*. Kashyap's films reflect the male anxiety of woman becoming a subject in control of her sexuality. One of the key elements, as mentioned, of classic film noir, a femme fatale, is a source of evil—the Other both feared and desired—posing a threat to the hero's moral integrity and ontological identity. Such male-centric, anti-feminist themes seem to be dominant in neo-noir, as well as in the new Hindi cinema, although the latter often employs a critical rather than affirmative perspective. Anurag Kashyap's *Dev D* is a good example.

Dev D

Kashyap takes a classic story of the self-destructive Devdas and—while performing an act of cultural translation and reworking and rewriting the cultural symbols of early 20th-century Bengal into early 21st-century global India—produces an acute and sometimes comic take on contemporary urban Indian masculinity. In the process of cultural translation, hybrid spaces emerge, where Paro masturbates while talking on the phone with Dev, who is studying in London; where Leni/Chanda (Chandramukhi [Kalki Koechlin]) is a schoolgirl giving a blow job to her boyfriend who films the act with his smart phone and later disseminates the video as an MMS. *Devdas* is translated into a neo-noir and to a large extent, a dirty realist film. A classic literary and cinematic text is placed into an ambivalent space in-between the past and present. Transculturality is brought into the classic text, and in the process, it transforms it.

Dev, or Devendra Singh Dhillon (Abhay Deol), son of a wealthy man from a small town in Punjab, is a noir and dirty realist anti-hero, a heavily drinking, heavily smoking *macho* man with "a transformed identity", as others say about him, and Paro (Mahie Gill) is his threatening femme fatale. She is his symptom, his object of desire, objet petit a, which is taken away from him, causing a massive trauma. Dev's rejection of Paro after a rumor spreads that she sleeps around with everyone very clearly illustrates the anxiety caused by getting close to the object of desire and desperate attempts to "bend" the space so as to permanently delay the attainment of the object. In this case, the object is a woman, and this fact among others makes this story a critique of masculine protest. The rejected Paro marries Bhuvan, a rich businessman from Delhi. Dev, who is experiencing a jouissance from the fact that he managed to keep his object distant, is spiraling down into self-destruction and the Delhi underbelly of brothels, drugs, thugs and illegal night bars. He gets pleasure from pain and self-inflicted torture. He rejects Paro, but is close to her physically. He observes her through a spyglass as a voyeur, and uses Rasika (Parakh Madan), Bhuvan's sister (with whom he has sex at the beginning of the film as a revenge on Paro) to get closer to Paro. Rasika tells Dev: "All you wanna do is fuck", to which Dev replies "Don't you?"

Dev does not care about Rasika; he does not care about Paro and not even about Chanda. He is a spoilt rich kid from rural Punjab, who goes on to study in London, transforming into a global desi. Kashyap's global desi is starkly different from similar heroes of the 1990s, especially the ones played by Shah Rukh Khan, who, incidentally, played Devdas in Sanjay Leela Bhansali's *Devdas* in 2002, several years before *Dev D* was released. In conflict with his father, unsure about his own desires, he develops what Freud called a castration complex or a masculine protest after coming back to India after completing his education in London. He is at the center of Kashyap's narrative while all the other characters, including the woman he *thinks* he loves as well as those women who care about him, are objects aiding his enjoyment. To enjoy—this is the only thing Dev wants, and what can be more enjoyable than jouissance, an orgasmic pleasure in pain.

Žižek (2007: 176–7), in explaining Lacan's thesis that woman is a symptom of a man, looks at Freud's concept of symptom, and the anti-feminist position of Otto Weininger, who claimed, according to Žižek, that "woman is nothing but materialization, an embodiment of man's sin" (as cited in Žižek 2007: 175). A woman exists "insofar as she attracted the male gaze" (Žižek 2007: 176). A woman in such a universe does not exist in herself as a subject; she exists only in the male gaze. Looking at noir and some cases of dirty realist imaginary, we can claim as Žižek (2007: 176) does, that a "woman is not an external, active cause which lures the man into a fall—she is just a consequence, a result, a materialization of man's fall". For this reason, Lacan (1999:72) announces that a woman does not exist. Paro as the ideal woman does not exist: she is the mirror for the narcissistic self of Dev and is the object of desire as long as she is unattainable. Žižek refers to Freud's classic formulation in his discussion on a woman: "the psychical value of erotic needs is reduced as soon as their satisfaction becomes easy" (as quoted in Žižek 2005: 94). The narcissistic self then creates artificial obstacles preventing the attainment of the object, or in other words, preventing the satisfaction, which is an illusion in the first place—the satisfaction lies in the impossibility of it. Coming too close to satisfying one's desires annihilates the desire itself. Žižek (2007: 178), following

Freud, states that a woman-as-ideal as opposed to a real woman transforms into the terrifying Otherness, or a Thing (Freud's *das Ding*).

Expressions of sexuality by a woman make her a slut, as *Dev D*
clearly demonstrates. Paro masturbates while on the phone with Dev.
She, upon his request, sends him naked pictures of herself. When Dev
opens her e-mail and sees her photo, there is no enjoyment as such in
the look on his face. Perhaps a very mild disgust, but more than that—
fear. Although he then calls Paro and announces that he is coming
back, his facial expression just prior to that says more. When he hears a
rumor about Paro, he is disgusted with her and calls her a slut. Rasika, a
Delhiite urban girl who has sex with Dev during Dev's "protest" against
Paro's strong femininity, is also projected as a slut who does not have to
be respected and who is always already a fulfiller of male desires. Dev
does not succeed in having sex with Paro, so Rasika is brought in as a
substitute, used and then remembered only when needed to perform
a certain function. She asks Dev, frustrated, "Do you even care about
me?" He does not reply, because he does not care about anyone but
himself. As Chunni the pimp tells Dev when they meet in Delhi, "In
Delhi, use the girls, but never keep them."

Sex is a complicated problem, and not only in *Dev D*, but in many
of Kashyap's films. Lack of it presents a problem and frustration, but
is it not the lack that is desired, not the object of desire? Dev does not
want to have sex with Paro. He needs to keep her as his objet petit a, at
a distance. That's why their making out is constantly interrupted—her
father always comes at the wrong moment. This interruption saves
Dev, because without the father, without "the name of the father" as
prohibition, to use a Lacanian notion, he probably would have to have
sex and would lose his object of desire. The rumor about Paro saves
him also, although, of course, everything is in the unconscious. On the
surface, we have his desire for Paro, his disgust, his *machismo*, while
in the unconscious, different processes are occurring related to his
own insecurity and instability as a man who is losing his control over
woman's sexuality, who is losing power. And because he cannot lose it,
on the conscious level, there are interruptions, accusations, distancing,
subsequent alcoholism, drug usage, etc. Dev cannot even have sex with

Chanda, a woman whom he purchases, as he is too drunk. He probably never has sex with her, nor are we shown any kind of physical intimacy between them. He has sex with Rasika unwillingly; sex in this case is a tool of power simply for Dev to demonstrate his manliness and his *potency* to Paro. Žižek (2005: 96) claims that "our 'official' desire is that we want to sleep with the Lady; whereas in truth, there is nothing we fear more than a Lady who might generously yield to this wish of ours—what we truly expect and want from the Lady is simply yet another ordeal, yet one more postponement". When postponements are exhausted and Paro takes a terrified Dev into the sugarcane fields to have sex, Dev runs away during the initial phase of lovemaking as there is nothing he fears more than sex with Paro. Over the years, since his early teens and his "exile" in London, he transformed Paro from a flesh-and-blood woman into a sublime object, a Thing looking at which one can only see the void, and hence, one has to always look sideways in order to not see the traumatic Thing in the place of what one consciously thinks is occupied by the beloved.

Conservative sentiments are also displayed in the story of how the schoolgirl Leni became Chanda the prostitute. Her parents are rich and urbane and her mother is Canadian, but their reaction is of a rigid patriarchal nature. Leni is sent to the Himalayan foothills to stay with her aunt. Her father kills himself out of pain and humiliation. She is then sent to her grandparents in Punjab, where a relative says that she should be killed as she brought shame on her family. There is also no shortage of sexual anxiety and fear/desire of a woman in films like *Ugly* or *Raman Raghav 2.0*.

Even though *Dev D* has strong elements of dirty realism, especially in the degradation of the main character, by rescuing him at the end of the film, Kashyap "destroys" the dirty realist narrative. In dirty realism, there is never a solution, there never can be emancipation and the character spirals down to hell becoming sub-human. Dev is about to reach this, but then Chanda "saves" him, and at the end of the film, they depart north, into the Himalayan foothills, with Paro left behind in each and every sense of the word. As I said before, dirty realism has certain thematic concerns—transforming social relations, cultural shifts and critique of capitalism, among other things. What could be called a *critique* or *presentation* of globality and transforming India is an important element in this film. Kashyap translates the classic story and populates it with "global" symbols. It is not accidental that when Dev is shown in London, in the background, there always are unmistakable symbols of London—Piccadilly Circus, a black cab, Houses of Parliament, etc. At a wedding party in India, he is dressed in a white shirt, tie and a waistcoat, as opposed to what is usually worn at such ceremonies. He is always with his iPod earphones. He drinks vodka. And of course, later in the film, there is no shortage of transculturality in Delhi. When Dev orders vodka and Coke at a bar, he is served vodka and Thums Up, a local variation of Coke. Chanda performs sex on a phone and speaks to a client seductively in four languages—English, Tamil, French, as well as Hindi. Chanda herself is half Indian and half Canadian.

In discussing Jameson's unrepresentability of the world of multinational capital, Bhabha (2004: 321), by drawing upon Walter Benjamin's idea of translation, speaks of migrant culture's untranslatability. Hybrid culture for him is a culture of survival, of *sur-vivre*, not the culture of arriving at a safe destination of binary dialectics of modern/traditional, or in our case, Western/ Indian or global/Indian. Hybrid culture in this sense is untranslatable and it is migrant in a symbolic sense of the word, by internalizing and reworking foreign cultural symbols by domesticating and vernacularizing them. "It is a strange stillness that defines the present in which the very *writing* of historical transformation becomes uncannily visible" (Bhabha 2004: 224). The transformation, both of social reality in neoliberal India and the imaginary, and the transformation of film forms and Hindi cinema overall have uncanniness weaved in the fabric of cultural newness.

A woman is a symptom of a man, Lacan told us. A man can only live through a woman, Žižek reminded us. A man can only survive/*sur-vivre* through a woman, and a woman in this case is the uncanny and the object of desire. She is an object/an Other through which a new man constructs his new self. This is Kashyap's interpretation of "newness entering India", newness that is sexual first and foremost. A woman who is desired, who is evil, who is a slut and who is the one and only who can satisfy male's desire. Such is the sexist brave new neoliberal world of "shining" Indian dystopia that Kashyap is presenting. But dystopia also relates to newness itself; newness can be dystopic due to its undecidability, instability and untranslatability. Perhaps that's why Dev is spiraling down into hell so fast, but at the last minute, Kashyap changes his mind and gives him a second chance—to live through, to sur-vive through another woman, who, in such a patriarchal logic, does not need to pretend what a woman really is—a slut. This is the no-arrival situation of Kashyap and his resolution. The "original" Devdas dies his Paro's doorstep. His "copy" a century later survives in order to continue the male-centric fantasy, where women are obedient, where sexuality is repressed, where the boundaries of interior/exterior are clear, where identities are uncomplicated, where one does not have to stare into the abyss and have it stare back; the abyss called the space in-between can be comfortably ignored.

Ugly

The first scene of Anurag Kashyap's *Ugly* (2013) is deeply unsettling and sets the tone for a bleak urban vision that is to come. A disheveled woman is in the bedroom. She sits on the bed with her back to the camera and looks at the mirror. Only her reflection in the mirror is visible to the spectators. The music helps to define the mood of the film—death metal—something very rarely used in Indian cinemas. In the scene, while the music plays, the woman moves toward a table, and there is a nearly empty whiskey glass on it. We understand that she drank it. She pours the remaining whiskey into a plate, pours some water in a glass and drops a dissolving Aspirin pill into it. She looks around the room, scared, as if there is a presence of something that should not be there, as if the room is uncanny, and sees a scarf hanging on a blade of the ceiling fan. All this while, death metal is playing. She goes into another room, goes to a cupboard, takes out a revolver from the drawer and places it into her mouth. There is a knock on the door. It is her 10-year-old daughter. The woman removes the revolver from her mouth and opens the door. And then the movie title appears, Ugly, in blood-red letters on a black background, and all this while disturbing music is playing. This scene is strikingly similar to Michael Haneke's opening scene of Funny Games (1998). The latter dirty realist film focuses on psychological violence, exposing a storm beneath the calm surface and darkness beneath a beautiful façade of middle-class life. A storm, the terrible future middle-class families have in store for them, alienation and social degradation are some of the recurring themes in Haneke's early films. There is another dirty realist aspect that relates Haneke's films to Ugly—the lack of care for children, alienation in the family between children and parents, and often, between a husband and wife. The disappearance of the girl is a result of the lack of care and of the fact that she was an unwanted child.

Violence in Dev D is self-inflicted, as if the man is punishing himself for not knowing what to be and how to be. Outward directed violence is an attempt to camouflage the feelings of inferiority, feelings of being "not manly enough". The elusive problem of "being a man", how to be one and what that means has been plaguing film noir from the inception. And the question of masculinity here should not necessarily be understood directly. In a more Adlerian sense, as I mentioned, "masculinity" here means power of any kind—physical as well as, and perhaps more importantly, economic, one of socio-economic status and this includes being rich and successful. Or, in other words, being the entrepreneur, inventing oneself, forcing oneself up the socio-economic ladder into the "middle classness" or "world classness". Titli, B.A. Pass and Moh Maya Money, which I discussed in the previous chapter, illustrate this problem quite well, without an emphasis on masculine protest.

Ugly, on the other hand, is a raw and violent film and has a far more pronounced masculine anxiety problem. For the most part, it focuses on a police investigation of the kidnapping of a young girl. But more than that, the film is about masculine insecurity, greed, desire to be successful and powerful, and of course, about the threat of strong femininity to the patriarchal status quo.

Shalini (Tejaswini Kolhapure), the woman in the first scene, and Rahul (Rahul Bhat) are divorced. Rahul is a struggling actor and used

to beat her when they were married. They have a daughter Kali. Shalini
and Kali were "saved" from the failing marriage, domestic violence and
poverty by a college friend Shoumik (Ronit Roy), who was in love with
Shalini back in those days, used to be bullied by Rahul while in college,
but now is a Mumbai police inspector—an influential, macho-type
man, violent, as such men usually are. In college, Rahul was a bully; he
was the powerful one vis-à-vis goofy Shoumik. But later in life, things
change drastically for them: Rahul is a struggling actor barely making
his ends meet. In several scenes, he is shown lifting weights in front
of a mirror, adoring himself. But his power, really, ends just there—his
masculinity is limited to his physique. Shoumik, on the other hand, is
a police inspector, a powerful figure with a license to beat and bully,
which he does often. He is also a provider; he and Shalini live in a cozy
middle-class apartment and have a servant, cars and no lack in material
comforts. But happiness is simply not there. Life is marked by the sense
of uncanny, something the first scene illustrates quite well. Shalini is
depressed and suicidal, and we never quite learn why. Both Rahul and
Shoumik are insecure in the face of a woman. Shalini leaves the violent
and poor Rahul for a middle-class life with Shoumik, who does not
trust his wife and dwells in his insecure world wiretapping his wife's
phone and listening to her phone conversations.

One Saturday, Rahul picks up Kali to spend a day with her, as it is
"his" day. He has to collect the hard copy of a film script from a friend
and leaves Kali alone in his car at a market in Andheri. Kali plays with
her iPhone, and attracts the attention of a man selling children's masks
and balloons. This is the last scene in which we see her. When Rahul
and his friend Chaitanya (Vineet Kumar Singh), who is also in film
business, come back to the car, she is gone.

The investigation, uncovering the dirt beneath a seemingly clean
middle-class living, ensues. But the real darkness, the ugliness and dirt
of the film, can be located in precisely the lack of care, excessive individuality, a strong desire for money and a desire to succeed in the dark
and brutal reality of a big city. The first-half of the film focuses on the
search for the missing girl, but in the second-half, Kali and the fact
that she disappeared goes into the background. Chaitanya decides to

pose as a kidnapper and calls Rahul and Shalini demanding ransom. While Rahul seems to be more concerned about his own rivalry with Shoumik, Shalini wants a new life away from both men, and here, the ransom money comes handy. In short, all characters are shown to be selfish, following their own agendas. At the end of the film, Kali's body is found very close to the market where she was kidnapped. She was tied up and hidden by the mask-selling man. As he was hit and killed by a truck during the chase at the beginning of the film and nobody truly knew he was the kidnapper, Kali died alone, tied up, likely out of hunger, heat and dehydration. In the last scene of the film, we are shown her body with maggots on her hands and her face.

The film evokes a fear of uncontrollable female sexuality and male impotence when faced with the fact of transforming sexualities and gender roles. Shoumik can be viewed as a classic noir hero—a hard-boiled, excessively macho police inspector whom everyone fears. But he taps his wife Shalini's phone and eavesdrops every day as he does not trust her. Or, in other words, mistrust comes from his own insecurity, which we can relate to his college days, when he was being bullied and laughed at by Shalini and Rahul. He compensates this trauma by being a tough cop and beating up arrested suspects, as well as commanding fear and respect from his subordinates. But his strength ends there; he feels powerless in his homely space and tries to exercise his "husband power" in not letting Shalini leave home and listening to her phone conversations. Hence, Shalini contemplates suicide. The interior of Shoumik's life is carefully hidden from the outside world; in the public space, he is as tough as it gets.

Rakhi (Surveen Chawla), Rahul's lover and Shalini's friend, could be seen as the opposite of Shalini. She demonstrates her sexuality and is what Shalini is not—seductive and scheming, using men but not getting too attached to them. In one scene, she changes her clothes in front of her estranged husband, while he trembles with lust watching her in nothing but underwear. After she is done, she comes over to him, grabs his crotch and says: "I see how much you love me." The man just stands there, unable to say or do anything. From this scene, we may get the feeling that her husband is impotent. Later, when she runs away with Rahul, she leaves a letter to her husband saying that she wanted to be with a man "who knows how to love". Impotence here is just symbolic; it represents a more social impotence and anxiety in the face of a woman and can be interpreted as a synonym of castration. Men in this film ultimately lose everything—women as well as their power. Even if they thought they had that power and were functioning in the patriarchal order, they are proved wrong. Shalini attempts to kill Shoumik but then leaves him. Rakhi leaves her husband, but ultimately leaves Rahul also. The men are castrated and left to their own lives and in their own worlds because of their inability to function in a transformed space.

An important element of the film is what Shaviro (2010: 19) called a "post-cinematic 'media ecology'"—an obsession with high-tech, gadgets, especially iPhones, wiretapping, online criminal databases. The kidnapped child has a pink iPhone which her mother gifted her. Shoumik's brother-in-law is an iPhone and iPad smuggler. At the beginning of the film, Shoumik is introduced to a major technological development at Mumbai police, a digital database where various data can be stored facilitating the search for people—personal data, bank account data and so on. Electronic gadgets, brands and the mediation of things mark the proliferation of "globality" and digitalization, but ultimately fail, as they are unable to provide any resolution to the film's problems. Kashyap is ironic in projecting globalizing India, and a fixation on the symbols of the emergent "global self"—Apple products, smart phones, digitalization of life—on mediated goods and brands that have become a part of everyday life in India. Writing on science fiction and high tech, Jameson (1996: 157) argues that "the interfusion of crowds of people among a high technological bazaar with its multitudinous nodal points, all of it sealed into an inside without an outside, which thereby intensifies the formerly urban to the point of becoming the unmappable system of late capitalism itself".

Such a position, with certain reservations, could be applied to my claims, although I believe that the capitalist system, while unrepresentable, is precisely mappable. Unrepresentability, affective mapping, antirealism—the negative connotations of these terms resonate in Hindi noir cinema, evoking anxiety of hybrid amorphous space where the clear-cut dualities and certainties are collapsing.

What is interesting and illustrates Kashyap's post-cinematic engagements is that prior to the film's official release, a short film *Kali-Katha* was released on YouTube—a prologue and a look at the circumstances in which Kali was conceived (in the film itself, this is not shown; we are only given clues). In this brief four-and-a-half-minute-long film, Shalini and Rahul are shown living in poverty, barely managing to get food. Shalini tells Rahul that she is hungry and she is afraid that she would not be able to manage this kind of life. Rahul is shown lifting weights in front of the mirror, admiring his muscles and photographs of himself. He dreams of becoming a film hero someday. On the shelves in the kitchenette, there are more imported bodybuilders' whey powder canisters than food. One night, Rahul gets drunk, and prompted by his friend Chaitanya to be a man, comes home, beats up Shalini and rapes her (although the rape is not actually shown). The caption after the last scene, just after Rahul takes off his jeans with the intention to rape his wife, reads: "... and Kali was conceived". Equally dark and disturbing, this short film is interesting not so much as a prologue, but as a post-cinematic event, in the sense that it was publicly released using social media—itself a marker of globalizing neoliberal India. Also, Kashyap's first film *Paanch* was also released only on YouTube. This correlates with the constant and often ironic references to technology and usage of it in the film itself.

Raman Raghav 2.0

Raman Raghav 2.0 can be seen as a continuation of the themes explored in *Ugly*. While in *Ugly*, the everyday life was very easily destabilized by a tragic event, undoing the lives of everyone involved, in *Raman Raghav 2.0*, the everyday life is already in ruins. The dark city already possesses the souls of all dwelling in it. Set in a dark and disturbing Mumbai, a city which is one of the central protagonists in this film, it focuses on a junkie police officer Raghav (Vicky Kaushal), highly troubled, homicidal and suicidal, who is trying and constantly failing to catch a serial killer named Raman (Nawazuddin Siddiqui). The latter becomes Raghav's archenemy, and in many ways, his double. The film is loosely based on Raman Raghav (real name, Sindhi Dalwai), a serial killer who terrorized Bombay in the 1960s, and who later was caught and sentenced to life imprisonment. Raman in the film admits he is inspired by the real-life Raman Raghav. In the film, he, a seemingly homeless man, roams around Mumbai killing people with no apparent reason except for playing a cat-and-mouse game with the police. He is an urban flâneur and seems to be taking sheer pleasure both in killing and in the city itself; he is, ambiguously, both homeless and not, as the city itself is his home and he is a product of it and of its history. Thus, Kashyap offers a peculiar flânèrie through the dark city, through alienation and meaningless violence, and most importantly, through self-destruction and hatred for women, which seems to arise due to social and spatial deconnection.

While Raghav is a depressed and violent cop, clearly demonstrating masculine protest, Raman, his alter ego, is an effeminate homme fatal. But here *Raman Raghav 2.0* strongly departs from all conventions. The relationship between Raman and Raghav is very similar to this, and I would say that their relationship demonstrates quite a lot of homosexual tendencies. "You have been searching for your freedom in a woman", tells Raman to Raghav at the end of the film, while in police custody. Real freedom, according to Raman, was for Raghav to become one with Raman—a path to self-discovery, which is self-destruction. "Becoming one" could, of course, be interpreted differently, but the sexual reference is very clear. Raghav should stop in his pursuit of a woman and become what he should be, what he almost was destined to be—a killer on his path to self-destruction. Becoming Raman here means not only becoming a murderer, not only embracing his own dark side, but also the end of desire. Raman is asexual throughout the film; there are no sexual references related to him. In his appearance too, he seems to be quite effeminate. Raghav, on the other hand, seems to be a macho man—tough, good looking, always dressed stylishly, always wearing Ray-Ban sunglasses. Raman as homme fatal manages to pose an existential threat to his pursuer, but at the same time, offers a salvation and a solution to the existential dilemma—to become what one was meant to become. Raman tells him that what he has never seen is a noose a man makes for himself. Here, he refers to Raghav, who, in the course of the film, has spiraled down into the bottom, becoming a murderer. At the same time, self-destruction also means the inability to live, inability to accept life as it is. Why is Raghav violent and depressive? This question without a clear answer is ever present throughout the film. What are the origins of his *condition*? Unresolved Oedipal complex is one possible answer. In one scene, Raghav comes to his parents' house. He is high on drugs and is wearing sunglasses in order to conceal his blood-shot eyes. His father confronts him and starts scolding him, to which Raghav reacts very violently and nearly punches his father. The film does not elaborate on Raghav's relationship with his parents, but from this scene, it is clear that he has had serious problems with the authoritative father figure and is what we could call a "failed son". As I mentioned before, both him and Dev from *Dev D* could be interpreted as sons who want to break out of from the shadows of their fathers and seemingly succeed only to spiral into the bottom, unable to resolve their Oedipal complex, unable to function in any meaningful relationship with a woman, and directing violence, either physical or mental, toward themselves and others.

In a scene at the end of the film, Raghav meets a girl, Ankita, at a nightclub and brings her to Simmy's apartment, where he lives, to his girlfriend's utter dismay. In the elevator, while reaching home, he takes a Viagra pill. When Simmy opens the door, Raghav pushes her aside and takes Ankita to the bedroom, where he attempts to have sex with her but is unable to. Even Viagra does not help and Ankita laughs at him. Once again, his masculinity is threatened, challenged. Here, as in *Ugly*, the macho man is shown to be impotent on many levels. Although his physical "impotence" is caused by drugs, the desperate attempts to control women are in vain; he feels socially impotent as his one and only way to assert himself is through traditional masculinity where his position as a male is unchallenged. In a fit of anger, he leaves the room locking Ankita inside. Simmy is angry at him and he is looking for his drugs that he kept in a drawer in the living room. It is not there.

Simmy tells him she threw it away. "Don't talk to me like my dad", he says to Simmy. During a fight, Raghav screams, "Don't talk to me in a patronizing tone", and hits Simmy. She falls on a glass-top table and is fatally injured. Raghav kills the woman who dared to challenge him, and he could be interpreted as the "ideal" type of extremely insecure man, who inflicts violence on himself and on others on the way to his destination, which is nothing else but self-destruction. Masculine protest, therefore, can be interpreted as leading to man's self-destruction. *Dev D* dealt with jouissance quite explicitly, but there is little of it in Raghav. More than that, we are presented with a depressive and meaningless existence and inability to transform the self in social and cultural circumstances that have drastically shifted. What remains for such a man is to become his alter ego, someone who was always there, dormant—an annihilator.

In addition to all this, the problems forming the background of *Raman Raghav 2.0* include—the dark and brutal city, an uncanny transforming and growing space, increasing alienation and transformations rapid to the point that they become *unrepresentable* and only *mappable*. In the film, as well as in many others that are part of the new film form, we find, we are shown things we may wish to be ignorant about, and with each layer uncovered, we, together with the film characters, take a spiraling trip down into the unconscious of dark and dirty urban interiors, into spaces populated by the unseen beings, by desiring men and women, by horrific secrets and lies. There is also no shortage of dark spaces of the city, often shown at night—bars, night clubs, street food stalls selling cheap food, cheap eateries where the marginal ones, the penniless aspiring film heroes drink and dream of a different life. There are also claustrophobic police stations and illegal "secret" interrogation rooms in the middle of police colonies where the arrested ones are beaten up and tortured in order for them to confess to the crimes they committed and the ones they did not commit. Repressed sexual anxieties, suicidal behavior, unloved children growing up in spaces that are in a permanent state of crisis. Crammed, suffocating interiors of cheap dwellings, where men try to negotiate their sexuality and demonstrate their potency. Kashyap intervenes into such everyday life with his dystopic vision of the urban uncanny and, in doing so, draws an anti-realist, excessive map of the unconscious, which is always a hidden interior, and the act of exposing the interior, of blurring the line separating the interior from the exterior, can expose dirt and indeed be *ugly*. Kashyap in his work presents a dirty vision of urban India—excessive, anti-realist and anti-esthetic, unrepresentable. His film noir and dirty realism is a mental map of the dark side of transforming neoliberal India and of those dwelling on the margins, as well as those successful ones harboring darkness and dirt inside.

BIBLIOGRAPHY

Abbas, Ackbar. 2008. "Faking Globalization." In *Other Cities, Other Worlds: Urban Imaginaries in a Globalizing Age*, edited by Andreas Huyssen, pp. 243–64. Durham, NC and London: Duke University Press.

Abbott, Megan E. 2002. *The Street Was Mine: White Masculinity in Hardboiled Fiction and Film Noir*. New York: Palgrave Macmillan.

Adler, Alfred. 1956. *The Individual Psychology of Alfred Adler: A Systematic Presentation in Selection from His Writings*, edited by Heinz L. Ansbacher and Rowena R. Ansbacher. New York: Basic Books.

Adorno, Theodor W. 2005. *Minima Moralia: Reflections on a Damaged Life*. London: Verso.

Agamben, Giorgio. 1998. *Homo Sacer: Sovereign Power and Bare Life*. Stanford: Stanford University Press.

———. 2013. "On the Uses and Advantages of Living among Specters." In *The Spectralities Reader: Ghosts and Haunting in Contemporary Cultural Theory*, edited by Maria del Pilar Blanco and Esther Peeren, pp. 473–9. London: Bloomsbury.

Althusser, Louis. 1971. "Ideology and Ideological State Apparatuses." In *Lenin and Philosophy and Other Essays*, pp. 121–73. New York: Monthly Review Books.

Arvidsson, Adam. 2005. *Brands: Meaning and Value in Media Culture*. London and New York: Routledge.

Athique, Adrian and Douglas Hill. 2010. *The Multiplex in India: A Cultural Economy of Urban Leisure*. London: Routledge.

Augé, Marc. 2008. *Non-Places: An Introduction to an Anthropology of Supermodernity*. London and New York: Verso.

Bachelard, Gaston. 1994. *The Poetics of Space*, translated by Maria Jolas. Boston: Beacon Press.

Bakhtin, Mikhail. 1981. "Forms of Time and Chronotope in the Novel." In *The Dialogic Imagination*, edited by Michael Holquist, translated by Caryl Emerson and Michael Holquist, pp. 84–258. Austin: University of Texas Press.

Baudrillard, Jean. 1994. *Simulacra and Simulation*, translated by Sheila Faria Glaser. Ann Arbor: University of Michigan Press.

Bauman, Zygmunt. 2000. *Liquid Modernity*. Cambridge: Polity.

———. 2004. *Wasted Lives: Modernity and Its Outcasts*. Cambridge: Polity Press.

Benjamin, Walter. 2006. *The Writer of Modern Life: Essays on Charles Baudelaire*. Cambridge, Massachusetts and London: The Belknap Press of Harvard University Press.

Berman, Marshall. 2010. *All That Is Solid Melts into Air: The Experience of Modernity*. London: Verso.

Bhabha, Homi K. 2004. *The Location of Culture*. London: Routledge.

Bloch, Ernst. 1988. "Building in Empty Spaces." In *The Utopian Function of Art and Literature: Selected Essays*, translated by Jack Zipes and Frank Mecklenburg, pp. 186–99. Cambridge, Massachusetts: MIT Press.

Bourdieu, Pierre. 1977. *Outline of a Theory of Practice*. Translated by R. Nice. Cambridge, Massachusetts: MIT Press.

Brosius, Christiane. 2013. "'Enclave Gaze': Images and Imaginary of Neoliberal Lifestyle in New Delhi." In *Images That Move*, edited by Patsy Spyer and Mary Steedly, pp. 73–99. Santa Fe: School for Advanced Research Press.

———. 2014. *India's Middle Class: New Forms of Urban Leisure, Consumption and Prosperity*. New Delhi: Routledge.

Brown, Wendy. 2003. "Neo-Liberalism and the End of Liberal Democracy." *Theory and Event* 7(1). Available at http://muse.jhu.edu/journals/theory_and_event/v007/7.1brown.html; accessed on 23 February 2019.

———. 2015. *Undoing the Demos: Neoliberalism's Stealth Revolution*. New York: MIT Press.

Burgin, Victor. 1991. "Paranoiac Space." *Visual Anthropology Review* 7(2): 22–30.

Carrigan, Tim, Bob Connell, and John Lee. 1985. "Toward a New Sociology of Masculinity." *Theory and Society* 14(5): 551–604.

Certeau, Michel de. 1998. "Ghosts in the City." In *The Practice of Everyday Life. Volume 2: Living and Cooking*, edited by Michel de Certeau, Luce Giard, and Pierre Mayol, pp. 133–44. Minneapolis: University of Minnesota Press.

Cheung, Esther M.K. 2009. *Fruit Chan's Made in Hong Kong*. Hong Kong: Hong Kong University Press.

Comaroff, Jean and John L. Comaroff. 2001. "First Thoughts on A Second Coming." In *Millennial Capitalism and the Culture of Neoliberalism*, edited by Jean Comaroff and John L. Comaroff, 1–57. Durham, NC: Duke University Press.

Connell, R.W. 2005. *Masculinities*. Berkeley and Los Angeles: University of California Press.

Dardot, Pierre and Christian Laval. 2014. *The New Way of the World: On Neoliberal Society*, translated by Gregory Elliot. London and New York: Verso Books.

Davies, William. 2014. *The Limits of Neoliberalism: Authority, Sovereignty and the Logic of Competition*. London: SAGE.

Deleuze, Gilles. 2005. *Cinema I: The Movement Image*, translated by Hugh Tomlinson and Barbara Habberjam. London: Continuum.

Deleuze, Gilles and Felix Guattari. 2004. *Anti-Oedipus*, translated by Robert Hurley, Mark Seem and Helen R. Lane. London: Continuum.

———. 2013. *A Thousand Plateaus*. London: Bloomsbury.

Derrida, Jacques. 1981. *Dissemination*. Chicago: University of Chicago Press.

———. 2006. *Specters of Marx*. London and New York: Routledge.

Desser, David. 2003. "Global Noir: Genre Film in the Age of Transnationalism." In *Film Genre Reader III*, edited by Barry Keith Grant, pp. 516–37. Austin: University of Texas Press.

Devasundaram, Ashvin Immanuel. 2016. *India's New Independent Cinema: Rise of the Hybrid*. New York: Routledge.

Dhusiya, Mithuraaj. 2018. *Indian Horror Cinema: (En)gendering the Monstrous*. New York: Routledge.

Dimendberg, Edward. 2004. *Film Noir and the Spaces of Modernity*. Cambridge, Massachusetts: Harvard University Press.

Dixon, Wheeler Winston. 2009. *Film Noir and the Cinema of Paranoia*. Edinburgh: Edinburgh University Press.

Dwyer, Rachel. 2006. "Bollywood Bourgeois." *India International Centre Quarterly* 33(3/4): 222–31.

———. 2013. "Zara Hatke ('Somewhat Different'): The New Middle Classes and the Changing Forms of Hindi Cinema." In *Being Middle-Class in India: A Way of Life*, edited by Henrike Donner, pp. 184–209. London and New York: Routledge.

———. 2016. "Mumbai Middlebrow: Ways of Thinking about the Middle Ground in Hindi Cinema." In *Middlebrow Cinema*, edited by Sally Faulkner, pp. 51–68. London and New York: Routledge.

Featherstone, Mike. 2007. *Consumer Culture and Postmodernism*. London: SAGE.

Fernandes, Leela. 2006. *India's New Middle Class: Democratic Politics in an Era of Economic Reform*. Minneapolis: University of Minnesota Press.

Fisher, Mark. 2009. *Capitalist Realism: Is There No Alternative?* Winchester, UK and Washington, USA: Zero Books.

———. 2012. "What Is Hauntology?" *Film Quarterly* 66(1): 16–24.

———. 2016. *The Weird and the Eerie*. London: Repeater.

Foucault, Michel. 2000. "Different Spaces." In *Aesthetics: Essential Works of Foucault 1954–1984*, edited by James D. Faubion, 2, pp. 175–85. London: Penguin.

———. 2006. *History of Madness*, translated by Jonathan Murphy and Jean Khalfa. London and New York: Routledge.

Freud, Sigmund. 1985. "The Uncanny." In *Art and Literature*, edited by Albert Dickson, 14, pp. 335–76. The Pelican Freud Library. Harmondsworth: Penguin Books.

———. 2012. *On Narcissism*, edited by Joseph Sandler, Ethel Spector Person, and Peter Fonagy. Contemporary Freud: Turning Points & Critical Issues. London: Karnac Books.

Friedberg, Anne. 1994. *Window Shopping: Cinema and the Postmodern*. Berkeley: University of California Press.

Frow, John. 1997. *Time and Commodity Culture: Essays on Cultural Theory and Postmodernity*. Oxford and New York: Oxford University Press.

Gehlawat, Ajay. 2015. *Twenty-First Century Bollywood*. New York: Routledge.

Gilmore, Richard. 2007. "The Dark Sublimity of Chinatown." In *The Philosophy of Neo-Noir*, edited by Mark T. Conard, pp. 119–36. Lexington: The University Press of Kentucky.

Gopal, Sangita. 2011. *Conjugations: Marriage and Form in New Bollywood Cinema*. Chicago and London: University of Chicago Press.

Gopalan, Lalitha. 2015. "Bombay Noir." *Journal of the Moving Image* 13: 64–90.

Gordon, Avery F. 2008. *Ghostly Matters: Haunting and the Sociological Imagination*. Minneapolis and London: University of Minnesota Press.

Graham, Seth. 2000. "Chernukha and Russian Film." *Studies in Slavic Cultures* 1: 9–27.

Groys, Boris. 2014. *On the New*, translated by G.M. Goshgarian. London: Verso Books.

Guattari, Felix. 2000. *The Three Ecologies*. London and New Brunswick: The Athlone Press.

Gupta, Akhil. 2012. *Red Tape: Bureaucracy, Structural Violence, and Poverty in India*. Durham, NC: Duke University Press.

Harvey, David. 1990. *The Condition of Postmodernity: An Enquiry into the Origins of Cultural Change*. Oxford: Blackwell.

———. 2007. *A Brief History of Neoliberalism*. Oxford and New York: Oxford University Press.

Heidegger, Martin. 1968. "Building Dwelling Thinking." In *Basic Writings of Martin Heidegger*, translated by A. Hofstadter, pp. 323–39. New York: Academic Press.

Inden, Ronald B. 2001. *Imagining India*. Bloomington: Indiana University Press.

Isin, Engin F. 2002. *Being Political: Genealogies of Citizenship*. Minneapolis and London: University of Minnesota Press.

———. 2004. "The Neurotic Citizen." *Citizenship Studies* 8(3): 217–35.

Jameson, Fredric. 1991. *Postmodernism, or, The Cultural Logic of Late Capitalism*. London: Verso.

———. 1994. *The Seeds of Time*. New York: Columbia University Press.

Jarvis, Brian. 2001. "How Dirty Is Jayne Anne Phillips?" *The Yearbook of English Studies* 31(1): 192–204.

Kaes, Anton. 2003. "A Stranger in the House: Fritz Lang's 'Fury' and the Cinema of Exile." *New German Critique* 89, Film and Exile: 33–58.

Khanna, Parul. 2013. "Anurag Kashyap, the Godfather". *Hindustan Times*, 9 July 2013. Available at http://www.hindustantimes.com/brunch/anurag-kashyap-the-godfather/story-SW0CUzKTN8ElmqC7WKjPxL.html; accessed on 23 April 2016.

Klein, Naomi. 2007. *The Shock Doctrine: The Rise of Disaster Capitalism*. London and New York: Allen Lane.

Koepnick, Lutz. 2002. *The Dark Mirror: German Cinema between Hitler and Hollywood*. Berkeley, Los Angeles, and London: University of California Press.

Krutnik, Frank. 1991. *In a Lonely Street: Film Noir, Genre, Masculinity*. London and New York: Routledge.

Lacan, Jacques. 1998. *The Four Fundamental Concepts of Psychoanalysis. The Seminar of Jacques Lacan*, Book XI, edited by Jacques-Alain Miller, translated by Alan Sheridan. New York and London: W.W. Norton & Company.

———. 1999. "On Feminine Sexuality, The Limits of Love and Knowledge. Encore." *The Seminar of Jacques Lacan*, Book XX, edited by Jacques-Alain Miller, translated by Bruce Fink. New York and London: W.W. Norton & Company

———. 2017. *Transference. The Seminar of Jacques Lacan*, Book VIII, edited by Jacques-Alain Miller, translated by Bruce Fink. Cambridge: Polity Press.

Lash, Scott and Celia Lury. 2007. *Global Culture Industry: The Mediation of Things*. Cambridge: Polity.

Lee, Joseph Tse-Hei and Satish Kolluri (eds). 2016. *Hong Kong and Bollywood: Globalization of Asian Cinemas*. New York: Palgrave Macmillan.

Lehman, Peter. 2007. *Running Scared: Masculinity and the Representation of the Male Body*. Detroit: Wayne State University Press.

León, Christian. 2005. *El Cine de La Marginalidad: Realismo Sucio y Violencia Urbana*. Quito: Universidad Andina Simon Bolivar.

Lewis, Tyson and Daniel Cho. 2006. "Home Is Where the Neurosis Is: A Topography of the Spatial Unconscious". *Cultural Critique* 1(Autumn): 69–91.

Lindop, Samantha. 2015. *Postfeminism and the Fatale Figure in Neo-Noir Cinema*. New York: Palgrave Macmillan.

Mankekar, Purnima. 1999a. "Brides Who Travel: Gender, Transnationalism and Nationalism in Hindi Film." *Positions* 7(3): 730–61.

———. 1999b. *Screening Culture, Viewing Politics: An Ethnography of Television, Womanhood, and Nation in Postcolonial India*. Durham, NC: Duke University Press.

Manzoni, Celina. 2011. "Violencia Escrituraria, Marginalidad y Nuevas Estéticas." *Hipertexto* 14(Summer): 57–70.

Marcuse, Herbert. 2002. *One-Dimensional Man: Studies in the Ideology of Advanced Industrial Society*. London: Routledge.

Mažeikis, Gintautas. 2015. "Purvinasis Realizmas Ir Nulinis Ideologijos Laipsnis." Doxa. 2015. Available at http://doxa.lt/purvinas-realizmas-ir-nulinis-ideologijos-laipsnis/; accessed on 23 February 2019.

Mazumdar, Ranjani. 2002. "Ruin and the Uncanny City: Memory, Despair and Death in Parinda." In *SARAI Reader 02: Cities of Everyday Life*, pp. 68–79. New Delhi and Amsterdam: CSDS.

———. 2007. *Bombay Cinema: An Archive of the City*. Minneapolis: University of Minnesota Press.

———. 2010. "Friction, Collision, and the Grotesque: The Dystopic Fragments of Bombay Cinema." In *Noir Urbanisms: Dystopic Images of the Modern*

City, edited by Gyan Prakash, pp. 150–84. Princeton: Princeton University Press.

Mazzarella, William. 2003. *Shoveling Smoke: Advertising and Globalization in Contemporary India*. Durham, NC: Duke University Press.

———. 2013. *Censorium: Cinema and the Open Edge of Mass Publicity*. Durham, NC and London: Duke University Press.

Mukhopadhyay, Bhaskar. 2012. *The Rumor of Globalization: Desecrating the Global from Vernacular Margins*. London: Hurst.

Mulvey, Laura. 1989. "Visual Pleasure and Narrative Cinema." In *Visual and Other Pleasures*, pp. 14–26. New York: Palgrave.

Nandy, Ashis. 1998. "Indian Popular Cinema as a Slum's Eye View of Politics". In *The Secret Politics of Our Desires: Innocence, Culpability and Indian Popular Cinema*, edited by Ashis Nandy, pp. 1–18. London: Zed Books.

———. 2007. *An Ambiguous Journey to the City: The Village and Other Odd Ruins of the Self in the Indian Imagination*. New Delhi and Oxford: Oxford University Press.

Naremore, James. 2008. *More Than Night: Film Noir in Its Contexts*. Berkeley: University of California Press.

Oliver, Kelly and Benigno Trigo. 2002. *Noir Anxiety*. Minneapolis: University of Minnesota Press.

Osteen, Mark. 2013. *Nightmare Alley: Film Noir and the American Dream*. Baltimore: Johns Hopkins University Press.

Oza, Rupal. 2006. *The Making of Neoliberal India: Nationalism, Gender, and the Paradoxes of Globalization*. London and New York: Routledge.

Parsons, Talcott. 1954. *Essays in Sociological Theory*. Glencoe, IL: The Free Press.

Paul, Abhijeet. 2016. "Infrastructures of the Grey: Asli/Naqli in a Mohalla Bazaar". In *Dislocating Globality: Deterritorialization, Difference and Resistance*, edited by Šarūnas Paunksnis, pp. 182–209. Leiden and Boston: Brill.

Paunksnis, Šarūnas. 2014. "One-Dimensional Cinema: India's New Imaginary Spaces." *Economic & Political Weekly* 49(17): 118–22.

———. 2015. "Postmodern Experience in India: Imaginary Subaltern Space and Cinema." *History and Sociology of South Asia* 1(9): 36–52.

———. 2015/2016. "India Darkly: Film Noir and Dirty Realism in Neoliberal India." *Zeitschrift für Indologie und Südasienstudien*, Band 32/33, pp. 299–321. Hempen Verlag: Bremen.

———. 2016a. "Into the Wild: Otherness, Desire, and Transforming Film Form in Hindi Cinema." *Archiv Orientalni: Journal of African and Asian Studies* 84/1(Spring): 139–58.

———— (ed.). 2016b. "Dreams of Other Space: Heterotopian Emplacements of the Global." In *Dislocating Globality: Deterritorialization, Difference and Resistance*, pp. 343–72. Leiden & Boston: Brill.

————. 2017. "Towards Neurotic Realism: Otherness, Subjectivity, and New Hindi Cinema." *South Asian Popular Culture* 15(1): 1–13.

Peeren, Esther. 2014. *The Spectral Metaphor: Living Ghosts and the Agency of Invisibility*. London and New York: Palgrave Macmillan.

Petro, Patrice. 1989. *Joyless Streets: Women and Melodramatic Representation in Weimar Germany*. Princeton, NJ: Princeton University Press.

Prakash, Gyan. 2010. *Mumbai Fables*. Princeton, NJ: Princeton University Press.

Prasad, M. Madhava. 2000. *Ideology of the Hindi Film: A Historical Construction*. Delhi and New York: Oxford University Press.

————. 2007. "Realism and Fantasy in Representations of Metropolitan Life in Indian Cinema." In *City Flicks: Indian Cinema and the Urban Experience*, edited by Preben Kaarsholm, pp. 82–98. Kolkata: Seagull.

Rajagopal, Arvind. 2001. "Thinking About the New Indian Middle Class: Gender, Advertising and Politics in an Age of Globalisation." In *Signposts: Gender Issues in Post-Independence India*, edited by Rajeswari Sunder Rajan, pp. 57–99. New Brunswick, NJ: Rutgers University Press.

————. 2008. *Politics after Television: Hindu Nationalism and the Reshaping of the Public in India*. Cambridge, UK and New York: Cambridge University Press.

Rancière, Jacques. 2009. *The Emancipated Spectator*, translated by Gregory Elliot. London: Verso.

Ritzer, George. 2001. *Explorations in the Sociology of Consumption: Fast Food, Credit Cards and Casinos*. London: SAGE.

Said, Edward W. 1978. *Orientalism*. New York: Pantheon Books.

Segal, Lynne. 2007. *Slow Motion: Changing Masculinities, Changing Men*, third edition. New York: Palgrave Macmillan.

Sen, Meheli. 2017. *Haunting Bollywood: Gender, Genre, and the Supernatural in Hindi Commercial Cinema*. Austin: University of Texas Press.

Shaviro, Steven. 2010. *Post Cinematic Affect*. Winchester, UK and Washington, USA: Zero Books.

————. 2015. *No Speed Limit: Three Essays on Accelerationism*. Minneapolis: University of Minnesota Press.

————. 2016. "Post-Continuity: An Introduction." In *Post Cinema: Theorizing 21st-Century Film*, edited by Shane Denson and Julia Leyda, pp. 51–64. Falmer: Reframe.

Shields, Rob. 1991. *Places on the Margin: Alternative Geographies of Modernity*. London and New York: Routledge.

Smith, Ian Robert. 2013. "Oldboy Goes to Bollywood: Zinda and the Transnational Appropriation of South Korean 'Extreme' Cinema." In *Korean Horror Cinema*, edited by Alison Peirse and Daniel Martin, pp. 187–99. Edinburgh: Edinburgh University Press.

Sobchack, Vivian. 1998. "Lounge Time: Postwar Crises and the Chronotope of Film Noir." In *Refiguring American Film Genres: History and Theory*, edited by Nick Browne, pp. 129–70. Berkeley, Los Angeles, and London: University of California Press.

Spivak, Gayatri Chakravorty. 1995. "Ghostwriting." *Diacritics* 25(2): 64–84.

———. 2010. "Can the Subaltern Speak?" In *Can the Subaltern Speak?: Reflections on the History of an Idea*, edited by Rosalind C. Morris, pp. 237–91. New York: Columbia University Press.

Srivastava, Sanjay. 2007. *Passionate Modernity: Sexuality, Class, and Consumption in India*. New Delhi: Routledge.

———. 2014. *Entangled Urbanism: Slum, Gated Community and Shopping Mall in Delhi and Gurgaon*. New Delhi: Oxford University Press.

Standing, Guy. 2011. *The Precariat: The New Dangerous Class*. London and New York: Bloomsbury.

Stiegler, Bernard. 2011. *The Decadence of Industrial Democracies*. Cambridge: Polity.

———. 2014. *Symbolic Misery: The Hyperindustrial Epoch Vol. 1*. Cambridge: Polity.

Sundaram, Ravi. 2010. *Pirate Modernity: Delhi's Media Urbanism*. New Delhi: Routledge.

Vasudevan, Ravi. 2010. *The Melodramatic Public: Film Form and Spectatorship in Indian Cinema*. Ranikhet: Permanent Black.

Vidler, Anthony. 1994. *The Architectural Uncanny: Essays in the Modern Unhomely*. Cambridge, Massachusetts: MIT Press.

Virilio, Paul. 2005. *Negative Horizon*, translated by Michael Degener. London and New York: Continuum.

———. 2008. *Open Sky*, translated by Julie Rose. London and New York: Verso.

———. 2009. *The Aesthetics of Disappearance*, translated by Philip Beitchman. Los Angeles: Semiotext(e).

———. 2012. *Lost Dimension*, translated by Daniel Moshenberg. Los Angeles: Semiotext(e).

Williams, Raymond. 1973. *The Country and the City*. New York: Oxford University Press.

Žižek, Slavoj. 2005. *The Metastases of Enjoyment: On Women and Causality*. London and New York: Verso Books.

———. 2007. *Enjoy Your Symptom!: Jacques Lacan in Hollywood and Out*. New York: Routledge.

———. 2008. *In Defense of Lost Causes*. London: Verso.

INDEX

ABOUT THE AUTHOR

Šarūnas Paunksnis teaches philosophy at the Faculty of Social Sciences, Arts and Humanities, Kaunas University of Technology, Lithuania. His main research areas include, but are not limited to, Indian cinema, media philosophy, postcolonial theory, globalization and cultural theory. He has edited a book titled *Dislocating Globality: Deterritorialization, Difference and Resistance* (2016).